Evolution of the

CAB-FORWARD FIRE TRUCK

Kent Parrish

Iconografix

Iconografix
PO Box 446
Hudson, Wisconsin 54016 USA

Library of Congress Control Number: 2010933428

ISBN-13: 978-1-58388-267-2
ISBN-10: 1-58388-267-7

10 11 12 13 14 15 6 5 4 3 2 1

Printed in China

On the cover: North Vernon, Indiana; 1955 American LaFrance 700; *Kent Parrish*
Jordan Fire Company – Waterford, Connecticut; 1984 Seagrave HB; *Glenn Vincent*
Red White and Blue, Colorado; 1977 Oshkosh L/Pierce LTI 100'; *Dennis J. Maag*
Alexandria, Kentucky; 2009 Spartan Gladiator Classic/Summit Fire Apparatus; *Kent Parrish*

BOOK PROPOSALS

Iconografix is a publishing company specializing in books for transportation enthusiasts. We publish in a number of different areas, including Automobiles, Auto Racing, Buses, Construction Equipment, Emergency Equipment, Farming Equipment, Railroads & Trucks. The Iconografix imprint is constantly growing and expanding into new subject areas.

Authors, editors, and knowledgeable enthusiasts in the field of transportation history are invited to contact the Editorial Department at Iconografix, Inc., PO Box 446, Hudson, WI 54016.

www.iconografixinc.com

Table of Contents

Dedication

This book is dedicated to my wonderful wife, Kimberlie, and my beautiful children, Logan, Julia, and Evan, who have all learned to ignore me when I say "this will be my last book."

Acknowledgements

As always, the completion of this book would not have been possible without the diligent photography and documentation of many friends and fellow fire apparatus buffs over the decades. Credit is given with each image that appears in this book. Special appreciation is extended to the following people for their technical assistance, additional research, and simply going above and beyond – Tom Shand, Walt McCall, Chuck Madderom, Chris Cavette, Dennis Maag, John Gumbinger, and Roger Bjorge. Finally, I would like to pay respect to the late great Fred Crismon and thank his family for understanding "our" passion and ensuring his collection may live on in some form for the future benefit of us all.

Bibliography

Fire Engines Since 1990, by Walter M.P. McCall, Crestline Publishing, 1976

American LaFrance 700 Series 1945-1952 Volume 2 Photo Archive, by Lawrence E. Phillips, Iconografix, 2000

Maxim Fire Apparatus Photo History, by Howard T. Smith, Iconografix, 2004

Mack Fire Trucks, An Illustrated History 1911-2005, by Harvey Eckart, Iconografix, 2005

100 Years of American LaFrance, An Illustrated History, by Walter M.P. McCall, Iconografix, 2005

Seagrave: A Pictorial History of Seagrave Fire Apparatus, by Matthew Lee, revised and expanded edition, 2006

Illustrated Encyclopedia of American Fire Engine Manufacturers, by Walter M.P. McCall, Iconografix, 2007

Introduction

The *cab-forward* term has been widely used in the automotive industry – from trucking to passenger cars to locomotives. The concept was simply to maximize space for man and equipment while minimizing space for machine and improving functionality by pushing the cab farther towards the front than conventional design. However, the notion is equally correlated to cab placement versus engine location. Thus, other descriptors have included *cab-over, forward-control, cab-ahead, low cab-forward*, and *engine-forward*. Technically, the verbiage has become rather ambiguous. Loosely, the idiom has been applied to custom fire apparatus *in general* and *is* the embodiment of what we have come to know as the *quintessential* American fire truck.

Fire trucks are among the most specialized vehicles on the road. Even more extraordinary rigs such as airport apparatus and those built specifically for the military have utilized various cab-forward styles, but aren't indicative of universal fire apparatus evolution. Commercially available forward-control chassis have also routinely crossed over into fire apparatus – hence, "fire truck on a garbage truck chassis" – but aren't exclusive to the fire service and are generally grouped in the cab-over genre.

Therefore, the definition of *cab-forward* as related to fire apparatus in this particular examination can best be stated as a *"custom model primarily intended for general fire service application that features a cab placed substantially farther towards the front than conventional design with a vertical face absent of a traditional engine compartment with hood."*

The fire service cab-forward was conceptualized from early transit bus design; the study of which culminated in American-LaFrance pioneering the first cab-forward fire apparatus in 1938 with its compact JO/JOX service aerials. American-LaFrance then revolutionized the concept in 1945 with the *cab-ahead* of engine 700 Series, which incorporated rear-facing *jump seats*, a configuration known as the classic *canopy-cab* when fitted with a roof. Competition did not follow until the 1950s when the Crown Carriage Company and C.D. Beck Company, both firmly established in the bus industry, designed cab-forward fire apparatus.

The cab-forward introduced many benefits to the fire service. Load distribution was more balanced, which increased stability and improved handling. Steering was easier in traffic. More personnel could be safely seated. A proportionate wheelbase provided for more hose and equipment storage. Perhaps most importantly, forward visibility was increased. By the end of the 1950s most of the remaining major manufacturers had followed suit with their own cab-forward versions. Though long-nosed conventional models admirably soldiered on well past their prime, the paradigm shift had occurred.

The 1960s and 1970s saw the dawn of specialty truck manufacturers providing fire apparatus cabs and chassis to builders that did not have the means to design and construct their own or sought less costly production. Truck Cab Manufacturers (TCM) has provided its generic *Cincinnati Cab* and constructed exclusive cab shells for *everyone* in the fire apparatus business. Chassis providers have included the likes of International, Duplex, Hendrickson, Pemfab, and Spartan.

Aggressive manufacturers such as Pierce and Emergency One stole the industry in the 1980s with a slew of custom offerings that even gave commercial chassis a run for their money. We also saw the advent of tilt-cabs and more efficient engines, which pushed the motor compartment further into the front portion of the cab, resulting in a growing number of *engine-forward* models and the dilution of the *cab-forward* term. Also around this time, sadly, yet inevitably, the legendary names in fire apparatus began to fall.

The 1990s was one of rapid development for the fire service. New requirements from the National Fire Protection Association (NFPA) called for all firefighters to be enclosed, seated, and belted in all new fire apparatus. Specialty disciplines adopted by a still evolving fire service resulted in the prevalence of large multi-purpose cabs. New manufacturers had also rapidly risen to the forefront. And the new Millennium has seen chassis design driven, literally, by new Environmental Protection Agency (EPA) engine emissions standards.

The 21ˢᵗ Century fire engine has been rebuffed by classic enthusiasts as devoid of personality – a "shoe box on wheels." Function-over-form has taken precedent – operation, safety, ergonomics, comfort, and communications. However, there is no doubt that today's magnificent machines will acquire their own personas and followers in due time. Lest one forget the pioneering American-LaFrance JO/JOX was once hailed the "Ugly American."

Satirist Kurt Vonnegut once said *"I can think of no more stirring symbol of man's humanity to man than a fire engine."* The variance between terms – *cab-forward* or *engine-forward* – is vital for discussion and technicality, but really one-in-the-same regarding the evolution of an American classic.

American-LaFrance revolutionized the cab-forward fire apparatus. The timeless 700 Series is the epitome of the quintessential American fire engine. Madison, Indiana, operated this 1947 model with classic canopy cab and 1000-gpm pump. *Ron Heal*

Chapter 1:
The Pioneer and Revolutionary

Conventional – "conforming to accepted customs" or "using well-established styles." This had been *the* type of fire apparatus since the transition from horse power to *horsepower*. Natural evolution saw the placement of a motor in front of the driver, which resulted in the familiar long-nosed engine compartment with hood. While accepted as the norm, the flaws of conventional design would be argued by a manufacturer that was at the forefront of fire apparatus evolution.

The cab-forward concept has proven to be most beneficial for "local" use – delivery, garbage pick-up, and transit buses – an urban setting where functionality *is* the premium. These factors gave credence to the first notion of cab-forward fire apparatus. In the mid 1930s, John Grybos, of famed fire apparatus builder American-LaFrance, spent time in New York City riding transit buses to study the advantages of

forward-control on large vehicles in municipal traffic. His research and design culminated with the 1938 introduction of the straight-frame Model JO/JOX compact or *service* aerials – the first cab-forward fire apparatus built in America.

The ground-breaking art-deco design placed the driver *and* engine ahead of the front axle providing drastically improving handling and visibility. A wide semi-open cab featured a slender full-width windshield with small triangular quarter windows. Individual bucket seats for the driver and officer flanked each side of the engine compartment or *doghouse*. The cab flowed towards the rear enveloping the mid-mount aerial turntable. A siren was prominently mounted above the windshield and bug-eye headlights bulged out from each side of a two-piece mesh grille.

The American-LaFrance JO/JOX service aerial was the first cab-forward fire apparatus in America. Marietta, Ohio, received the first delivery in 1938 – a 65-foot model with exposed ladder bed and standard rear fenders. *Roger Bjorge collection*

The new aerials were offered in two distinct models. The "J" and "O" identified the Lycoming-derived J-Model V-12 engine and semi-open cab. The premium JO version came with a fully enclosed ladder bed and stylish teardrop rear fenders with hydraulically operated outriggers. The base JOX model had standard rear fenders and an exposed (hence the "X") ladder bank with a pair of manually operated outriggers that swung out from below the turntable. Both versions had an additional screw jack hidden underneath the front. Hydraulically operated three-section steel aerial ladders in 65, 75, 85, and 100-foot lengths would be offered.

As *the* rage in the 1930s was aerial ladder evolution, lost at first was the functionality of the fire chassis and cab. American-LaFrance loudly boasted of the benefits of its new compact design, even over its own tractor-drawn aerial. While the configuration was seen more as a complete style of fire apparatus, unprecedented forward visibility and overall maneuverability was certainly applicable to fire apparatus of all types – a fact that American-LaFrance would embrace.

With the advent of World War II, fire apparatus development in general was stifled. American-LaFrance and its competitors were left with no choice but to help with wartime production. Research and design generally took a backseat throughout the war years. The radical JO/JOX models continued to be delivered to the military, overseas, and to communities that were granted approval to receive new fire apparatus to protect efforts vital to defense. The

The American-LaFrance JO/JOX featured a forward motor compartment that was flanked by the driver and officer with the rear cab sheet metal enveloping the mid-mount aerial turntable. *Walt McCall collection*

compact aerials saw several minor running changes throughout its production run, which totaled a sum of 110 units.

Despite war, American-LaFrance had, in fact, already returned to the drawing board. For the International Association of Fire Chief's show, held in Chicago in 1943, American-LaFrance produced a 28-page booklet titled *The American-LaFrance Design Symposium on Motor Fire Apparatus* to survey ideals of postwar fire apparatus design. As it turned

The premium American-LaFrance JO version featured an enclosed ladder bank and hydraulic outriggers. This 75-footer went to Union City, New Jersey, in 1938. *Walt McCall collection*

The pioneering American-LaFrance JO/JOX provided improved handling and maximum forward visibility. Oswego, New York, received this 1939 JOX model with 75-foot ladder. *Walt McCall collection*

out, many of the principles were already being developed by American-LaFrance in a new, revolutionary cab-forward fire apparatus, which was already in the final design phase. The booklet even leaked subliminal hints as to what was to come with cartoon-like images of the design. The survey merely validated a nearly complete concept.

Throughout 1944, several clay styled models of the new proposed cab-forward design were evaluated. Included were a pumper, mid-mount aerial, and unbelievably, a rear-mounted aerial, a concept that would not be embraced by the American fire service for another 25 years. By 1945, two pilot-cars had been finished. The first was a 100-foot mid-mount aerial ladder with semi-open cab. The second was a pumper with a closed cab.

American-LaFrance was "all-in" with its new design. It immediately began advertising its revolutionary *Post War* 700 Series fire apparatus in fire service publications and even received attention from the early *Popular Science* magazine. The handsome model featured a narrow cab with two-piece V-type windshield and prominently mounted siren. Its face was defined by a chrome windsplit and bug-eye headlights. Noticeably absent was a front grille, as the motor compartment had been moved *behind* the front seat and axle, along with an oversized radiator, resulting in the *cab-ahead* of engine moniker. This arrangement allowed for seating for up to five – three up front and two facing rearward; one on each side of the doghouse in what would come to be known as *jump seats*, as a firefighter would jump onto the running board, spin, and slip into the seat. The 700 Series was available in two configurations – a semi-open style with quarter windows or as a closed cab with glass partition separating the front from the rear, the latter of which came to be known as the classic *canopy cab.*

Production of the JO/JOX aerials continued through 1946 while the plant was completely retooled

The American-LaFrance JO can't be mistaken for any other fire apparatus with its art deco cab and streamlined body. This 1940 model with 75-foot ladder went to Charleroi, Pennsylvania. *Roger Bjorge collection*

for the 700 Series, which began running in 1947. Factory records implied that the first 700 Series *delivery* went to Claymont, Delaware, but it is more widely accepted via company advertising that Elkhart, Indiana, actually received the first *two*.

The new 700 Series answered the chief complaints of having the engine in between the driver and officer – too much noise in the cab and difficult in accessing the motor during pumping operations. In addition, a choice of four V-12 engines was offered – Lycoming-derived F, G, and J models and the American-LaFrance E Series. Service aerials were available in 65, 85, and 100-foot heights in addition to 75, 85, and 100-foot tractor-drawn models. The 700 Series was also available in quadruple combinations, hose and booster cars, rescue and floodlight units, and even more specialized airport apparatus.

Many transportation buffs believe there are uncanny resemblances between the American-LaFrance 700 Series and the E/F-Series car-body locomotives of the Electro Motive Division (EMD) of General Motors of that time. This may be no coincidence as several rail lines ran near the Elmira plant, possibly providing an abundance of inspiration.

Despite all the rhetoric, there are "old-timers" who believe there was a bottom line resulting in the impetus for the 700 Series. The conventional 600 Series required costly amounts of sheet metal to cover the massive engine compartment and still provide for a cab. Possibly "proof in the pudding," orders were no longer accepted for the big conventional once tooling of the 700 Series line was complete.

Originally built for Lebanon, Pennsylvania, this 1940 American-LaFrance JO model with 75-foot ladder was preserved by the Mill Creek Fire Company in Marshalltown, Delaware, in its distinctive white and green scheme. *Shaun P. Ryan*

The rest of the fire apparatus industry, including chief competitors, criticized the cab-forward design, dubbing it a "suicide cab," as it was believed that placing the driver and officer up front would result in serious injuries in the event of a collision. American-LaFrance countered to the contrary. The new concept resulted in better weight distribution and less stress on the front axle, resulting in a 25-foot turning radius. Forward visibility had also increased by 250 percent. All of which would *decrease* collisions and injuries. The fire service itself seemingly agreed – as over three thousand 700 Series units were ordered over the next decade. It was merely a matter of time before the "competics" ate crow and jumped on the cab-forward bandwagon.

American-LaFrance built 110 JO/JOX service aerials. Production continued through World War II and into 1946. Sharon, Pennsylvania, received this JO model with 85-foot ladder in 1943. *Roger Bjorge collection*

The revolutionary American-LaFrance 700 Series not only boasted a new cab configuration, but was marketed as a completely new line of fire apparatus. *Fred Crismon collection*

In 1945, American-LaFrance announced its new cab-forward fire apparatus, which had already been on the drawing board when the fire service was surveyed two years earlier for its ideals on post war fire apparatus design. *Fred Crismon collection*

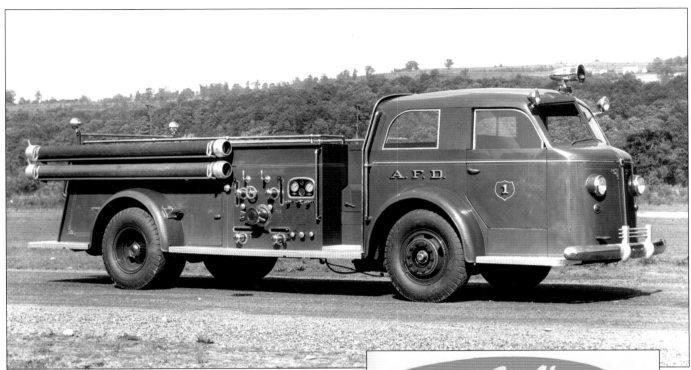

By 1945, American-LaFrance had built two 700 Series pilot cars, including a 1500-gpm pumper with canopy-cab lettered for the generic "Anytown Fire Department." It was put through the rigors of testing with the production version seeing exposed door hinges. *Walt McCall collection*

American-LaFrance had completely refined the cab-forward concept with the engine and a larger radiator being relocated behind the front axle allowing for three men up front and two in the rear-facing jump seats. *Walt McCall collection*

American-LaFrance was a loud advocate of the cab-forward concept, boasting its 700 Series offered 250% more vision than the conventional design. *Steve Hagy Collection*

American-LaFrance began full production of the 700 Series in 1947. The narrow cab featured a V-type windshield, no front grille, and windsplit with bug-eye headlights. Poughkeepsie, New York, received this 750-gpm pumper with semi-open cab and early plain bumper. *Walt McCall collection*

The layout of an American-LaFrance 700 Series pumper provided for more riding positions, increased equipment storage, and efficient hose storage – more space for man and equipment while minimizing machine. *Walt McCall collection*

The American-LaFrance 700 Series was available for all types of apparatus. New Brighton, Pennsylvania, received this city service ladder truck in 1948. Many believe the front end of the 700 Series was inspired by the new EMD locomotives of that time. *Steve Hagy collection*

The American-LaFrance 700 Series service aerials were even more efficient and refined than the JO/JOX versions. This 100-foot model went to Huntington, New York, in 1949. *Walt McCall collection*

Many traditional city departments still preferred tractor-drawn aerials. Geneva, New York, received this 1949 American-LaFrance 700 Series 100-foot Rescue Model with fixed tiller seat. *Kent Parrish collection*

In 1951, the Crown Firecoach became the first to challenge American-LaFrance in the cab-forward market. The pilot car with 1250-gpm main pump, 150-gpm auxiliary pump, and 350-gallon water tank served as a demonstrator until 1954, when it was purchased by West Covina, California, and is now collector owned. *Shaun P. Ryan*

Chapter 2: **The 1950s**

As the fire service entered the 1950s, it was still, as a whole, recovering from a lack of new equipment as a result of wartime production, and going back further, the economic woes of the Great Depression. Many communities were finally able to replace outdated equipment with the best rigs their money could buy and the fire apparatus industry was finally catching up on backlogs. American-LaFrance led the surge in the high end segment of a freshly robust market with peak production of its 700 Series.

The first to challenge American-LaFrance in the cab-forward segment was a surprise – certainly not one of the traditional names in fire apparatus up to that point – but not coincidentally, one with roots in the bus industry. The Crown Carriage Company of Los Angeles, California, dated back to 1904 and had primarily established itself as a builder of school buses. However, Crown had quietly begun building fire apparatus. As the school bus business was sea-

sonal, the firm decided to adapt its bus design for the fire service. Development began in 1949 and culminated in 1951 with the Crown Firecoach.

The pilot Firecoach was built on a modified forward-control International-Harvester chassis. Within two years, Crown was building on its own Z-frame chassis. Elevated up on the frame, pioneering a higher angle of approach, the Firecoach cab was distinguished by a smooth, slightly rounded face with a recessed siren hidden behind a circular, mesh grille. Claiming it was "not satisfied with the natural added visibility obtained by cab-forward design," Crown touted its extra large double curved windshield.

Crown epitomized *the* custom fire apparatus in its own advertising – "built from the ground up as a composite unit, designed expressly and wholly as a fire apparatus." The Firecoach also introduced innovations such as an auxiliary braking system, removable left front cab access panel, and an adjustable suspension system. Initially offered only with a semi-open configuration, a canopy cab was soon available. The self-proclaimed *Royalty of Fire Apparatus* was unique in that very few were sold east – it was a "West Coast rig," but a prolific one at that. The Firecoach was used for pumpers, manifold wagons, rescue squads, and aerials of all types.

In 1955, yet another shocking name, albeit a legendary one, announced a cab-forward fire apparatus. East Rutherford, New Jersey, was a faithful Ahrens Fox customer that wanted the visibility of the American-LaFrance 700 Series, but with the Ahrens Fox name. At their request, famed Ahrens Fox salesman and mechanic Frank Griesser collaborated with engineer Jim Beck of the Ohio-based C.D. Beck Bus Company, who had taken over construction of fire apparatus for Ahrens Fox. The end result was a new Ahrens Fox "FCB" pumper conceptualized from the cab of a Beck Greyhound bus – characterized by a curved front and wraparound lower steel band with recessed headlights. It was offered in both semi-open and canopy cab configurations, the latter of which featured a rounded roof.

Just a year later, trucking giant Mack purchased C.D. Beck with intent to position for a large intercity bus contract. However, Mack was so enamored with the Ahrens Fox cab-forward that they purchased the design rights and the crowning jewel presented as the first Mack model exclusive to fire apparatus. The renamed C-Series began production in 1957 and was available for all types of fire apparatus.

There *was* an interesting twist to the Ahrens Fox/Mack transition. Several Long Island, New York, departments wanted to purchase new or additional pumpers of the Ahrens Fox cab-forward design from Frank Griesser, but not under the Mack name. A side arrangement was made for local Approved Fire Equipment to build them. Approved, who even dropped the "E" in their logo so that it was reminiscent of Ahrens Fox, built a total of seven such rigs, which was actually one more than Ahrens Fox. Certainly the pact was questionable, but it was of no consequence as Mack eventually built 1,055 C-Series fire apparatus.

A reorganized American LaFrance Corporation had introduced a *new and improved* 800 Series in 1956. It could be differentiated by a standard left hand pump panel and compartmented body with angled running boards. Oddly, this series was

East Orange, New Jersey, received this big rescue squad built by American- LaFrance in 1950 on a 700 Series chassis with canopy cab. Such apparatus on early cab-forward chassis were quite rare. *Walt McCall collection*

The Westinghouse Electric Corporation maintained this classic 1951 American-LaFrance 700 Series 1000-gpm pumper with semi-open cab, lettered for its East Pittsburg Works in Pennsylvania. *Joel Gebet*

reserved for just the pumper line with the other types remaining under the 700 Series umbrella. The 800 Series was hastily conceived, cheaply built, and poorly received. American LaFrance saved faced by unveiling a completely re-engineered 900 Series, on which a full line would be available, in 1958. Sitting on a much deeper frame, it presented a cab that was a full eight inches wider with a wraparound windshield that was three inches higher. A face featured quad headlights and signals between horizontal trim bands. The hose body was four inches lower, providing a sleeker appearance.

American-LaFrance continued to tout the forward visibility of its apparatus over conventional design as illustrated in this advertisement. *Fred Crismon collection*

With this 1952 American-LaFrance 700 Series Rescue Model 100-foot tractor-drawn aerial for Tampa, Florida, not only did the driver have improved visibility, the tillerman could easily spot the front end of the apparatus. *Walt McCall collection*

Revered East Coast builder Maxim had begun development of their own cab-forward in 1958, with introduction a year later. The crisp, new "F" model would be the manufacturer's cab-forward mainstay for decades to come and was available for all types of apparatus. It was easily defined by quad headlights and signals complemented by a series of slim trim bands. The extremely roomy cab featured full width doors and a larger circular logo prominently displayed on the front. At the request of customers in the prolific sales territory of Indiana in conjunction with the presence of an International-Harvester plant, Maxim also built a handful of "CFX" engine-forward models with a front end reminiscent of the American LaFrance JO/JOX. Built on an International-Harvester bus chassis, it featured a full width

cab with long doors and bench seats facing each other in an unobstructed jump seat area.

In 1959, iconic Seagrave finally unveiled its first cab-forward after explaining away its perceived resistance to the concept as "months of engineering studies, research, and testing." The new "K" model featured a tall cab that measured 72 inches at the front door with a smooth face characterized by a siren recessed into the center and warning lights situated high, between slim trim bands. A standard Seagrave K model pumper was about two feet longer than a conventional Anniversary model. However, the wheelbase was a few inches shorter, highlighting a cab-forward advantage. Seagrave boasted its cab was the strongest and safest in the industry – a rigid structure consisting of safety-steel formed over all-welded square tubing on a special sub-frame. It was available in semi-open, canopy cab, and among the first to be regularly requested in a four-door, fully enclosed configuration. The lineup included KB pumpers, KA service aerials, and KT tractor-drawn aerials. In confirmation with conceptualization of the cab-forward, Seagrave old-timers reportedly quipped "we'll have to get *bus drivers* to deliver these damn things!"

Truck Cab Manufacturers (TCM) of Cincinnati, Ohio, traced its roots back to 1870 as the Highland Buggy Company. In 1948, John Weber, Sr., chief engineer of parent company Trailmobile, and a group of investors acquired the cab division and went into business as TCM, whose core business became designing and building specialty truck cabs, both generic and to customer specifications. In 1959, the Four Wheel Drive Corporation (FWD) celebrated its 50th Anniversary with the introduction of its Golden Fire Line, which included a new cab-forward version. Rather than invest in the design and construction of an entirely new model, FWD had subcontracted with TCM, who supplied a generic cab shell, which FWD installed on its own custom chassis and trimmed out for completion. The FWD cab-forward fire line consisted of "FF" series pumpers and "AF" series aerials – available in either two-wheel or full-time "Tractioneer" all-wheel-drive and to other body manufacturers.

Motive power for fire apparatus during this period remained gasoline driven engines from the likes of Waukesha and Hall-Scott coupled with manual transmissions. International-Harvester and Con-tinental also provided muscle. The Mack C-Series also boasted of its reliable Mack engines. However, a new age of power was coming.

The days of conventional models were numbered. As the 1950s came to a close, most of the big-name fire apparatus manufacturers had, begrudgingly or not, embraced the cab-forward concept and TCM had provided a ticket for the smaller builders to join the party. American LaFrance, the original pioneer, had become just another name on the guest list.

By 1953, Crown was building the Firecoach on its own Z-frame chassis and Los Angeles City had ordered the first of 149 units. This "triple combination" had a 1250-gpm main pump and a 250-gpm auxiliary pump, which was common in southern California and used in wildland firefighting. *Chuck Madderom*

The Crown Firecoach introduced innovations such as an auxiliary braking system, removable left front cab access panel, and an adjustable suspension system. Lynwood, California, operated this 1954 model with canopy cab. Note how the Crown pump panel was typically set farther back near the rear fender. *Chuck Madderom*

This 1954 model for Montecito, California, had a 1000-gpm pump, which was uncommon for Crown as the Firecoach was a "big city" pumper, typically with at least a 1250-gpm capacity. *Chuck Madderom*

The Crown Firecoach became a staple in firehouses all over the West Coast. A testament to its capabilities, Huntington Beach, California, operated this massive 1955 model with tandem axles, 1250-gpm main pump, 150-gpm auxiliary pump, and 2500-gallon water tank. Note the roof turret. *Chuck Madderom*

In 1956, American-LaFrance introduced the 800 Series pumpers, which were just warmed over versions of the 700 Series with compartmented bodies and angled running boards. St. Louis, Missouri, received nine of these 1000-gpm units with canopy cabs. *Fred Crismon collection*

The new American LaFrance 800 Series was reserved only for pumpers. All other types remained under the 700 Series umbrella. The U.S. Navy operated this 1956 700 Series with 85-foot service aerial. *Fred Crismon collection*

In 1955, legendary Ahrens Fox introduced a cab-forward pumper built by C.D. Beck and based on its Greyhound bus design. Only 6 units were delivered, with Northern Hills, Ohio, receiving the last, a 1956 model. The 750-gpm unit carried 400 gallons of water. *Steve Hagy*

American LaFrance introduced the completely re-engineered 900 Series in 1958 to recover from the poorly conceived and received 800 Series pumpers. Sitting on deeper frame rails with a cab that was 8 inches wider, the 900 Series featured a wraparound windshield and quad headlights. *Fred Crismon collection*

In 1957, Mack Trucks purchased C.D. Beck and acquired the Ahrens Fox cab-forward fire apparatus design, renaming it the C-Series, which began production in 1957 and was embraced by New York City with multiple large orders of pumpers, aerials, and satellite units during its production run. *Steve Hagy collection*

In a side arrangement and contrary to Mack purchasing the design rights, Approved Fire Apparatus built 7 pumpers of the Ahrens Fox cab-forward design for loyal East Coast customers. This 1958 model with a 1000-gpm pump and 500-gallon water tank found a second home in South Ogden, Utah. *Shaun P. Ryan*

The obvious visible difference of the Mack C-Series was the standard rear fenders as opposed to the compartmented and angular Ahrens Fox design. Los Angles City received a group of pumpers in 1958 with 1000-gpm pumps, 500-gallon water tanks, and Hall Scott gasoline engines. *Chuck Madderom*

The majority of early Crown Fire-coaches were built with semi-open cabs. An option, and typical later retrofit, was the addition of a simple canopy. Ventura City, California, operated this 1958 model with 1250-gpm pump, 500-gallon water tank, and Hall-Scott gasoline engine. *Chuck Madderom*

In 1959, Maxim introduced its F model cab-forward fire apparatus. The roomy cab featured full-width doors and distinctive Maxim appearance. South Bend, Indiana, received the first unit, built in 1958. *Howard Smith collection*

Maxim built a handful of CFX engine-forward fire apparatus for Indiana customers. Based on a locally-built International-Harvester bus chassis, the rear crew portion of the cab featured bench seats that faced each other. Units are known to have been delivered to Terre Haute, East Gary, and Connersville. *Kent Parrish collection*

In 1959, Seagrave concluded months of reported testing and research by finally unveiling its own cab-forward fire apparatus, the K models. The first delivery was this KB pumper for Jackson, Tennessee. *Fred Crismon collection*

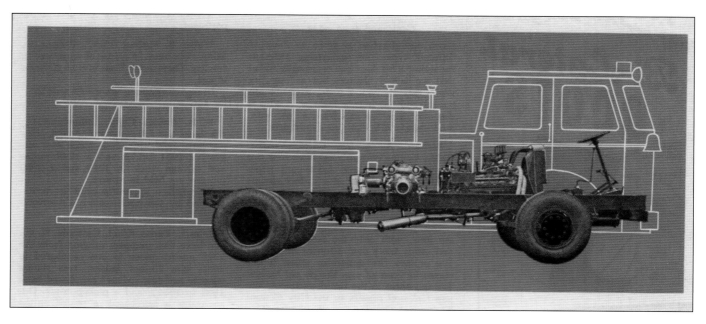

This illustration highlights the engine placement in not only a Seagrave, but a typical cab-ahead of engine fire apparatus. *Kent Parrish collection*

Seagrave boasted of the strongest and safest cab in the industry. This 1959 KB pumper delivered to Wauchula, Florida, displays the rear of the canopy portion. *Kent Parrish collection*

The Seagrave K models made an immediate impact in the fire service. Portland, Oregon, received a group of units, including this 1959 KT 100-foot tractor-drawn aerial with non-fixed tiller seat. *Kent Parrish collection*

FWD celebrated its 50th Anniversary in 1959 with the introduction of its Golden Fire Line, which included new cab-forward FF pumpers and AF aerials. FWD contracted with TCM, who built the cab shells, which were placed and trimmed out by FWD on its own chassis. *Fred Crismon collection*

Peter Pirsch finally introduced its own cab-forward in 1960. The "Safety Cab" was built by hand one at a time in Kenosha, Wisconsin. The canopy cab version featured a characteristic rear corner cutout with flowing grab rail. This 750-gpm unit with 750-gallon water tank was delivered to the suburb of Middleton. *John Javorsky/Chuck Madderom*

Chapter 3: The 1960s

As peace, love, and harmony swept through the 1960s, so did the cab-forward concept within the fire service. The cab-forward completely overran the venerable conventional models during the psychedelic period. In fact, by 1962, Seagrave cab-forward pumpers were outselling the conventional Anniversary Series pumpers 3 to 1. As further trends went, the 1960s was the decade of the Snorkel. Custom cab-forward chassis from FWD, Mack, and Maxim were popular choices early in the Pitman Snorkel campaign. Many manufacturers also began to delineate custom "fire trucks" from "road trucks" as *specifically for firefighting and firefighters with chassis built to stand-up under severe traffic and firefighting conditions.* Additional development included the increasing preference of protection from the elements which

resulted in an overwhelming transition to canopy cab configurations rather than the dated semi-open style. Other modern trends made even more functional by the cab-forward were extended front bumpers which accommodated front intakes and pre-connected suction lines.

The 1960s also saw the transition from gasoline to diesel engines and an astonishing alternative. The more efficient diesels simply powered larger apparatus and allowed higher pumping capacities. The change of muscle saw Caterpillar, Cummins, and Detroit Diesel come to prominence. American LaFrance's relevance during this decade wasn't a new chassis, but rather their experimentation with turbine powered fire apparatus. Featuring a Boeing Model 502-10C gas turbine engine and easily identified by a large stainless steel exhaust stack sprouting rearward out of the doghouse, two Turbo-Chief pumpers and a 100-foot tractor-drawn aerial were produced, but eventually converted to "normal" power after chronic problems.

Legendary builder Peter Pirsch finally introduced its own cab-forward fire apparatus in 1960. A pilot car had been built a year prior. The design featured a rather large cab that was narrowed down for the production models. Addressed properly as Semi (open) Cab-Forward and Canopy (closed) Cab-Forward, Pirsch also self-referenced its "Custom Built *Safety Cab*" in recognition of heavy gauge construction and 1/4-inch safety plate glass windows. No two cabs were precisely equal in measurement as each was formed by hand over a large jig in Pirsch's plant. The final design featured a handsomely distinctive appearance with the Pirsch logo prominently displayed on the front with a cutout and flowing grab rail at the upper rear corner of the canopy cab version.

Three West Coast manufacturers had also entered the cab-forward arena. Coast Fire Apparatus offered custom cab-forward pumpers from the late 1950s into the 1960s. It is believed their units were sculpted utilizing chassis with forward-control kits and cab sheet metal from International-Harvester. Westland Fire Apparatus built a few matching sets of cab-forward pumpers and Snorkels for Pacific Northwest departments during the early 1960s. Their Fireliner, which featured a distinctive five-man canopy cab with sloping front, is thought to have been fashioned using White-Freightliner forward-control chassis and sheet metal. Van Pelt had also designed and built its own Custom 300 cab-forward fire apparatus. While the pilot car was built with a Diamond T chassis kit, production units were built on Van Pelt's own frame.

In 1960, Ward LaFrance introduced its Firebrand pumper. Although certainly a cab-forward compared to its conventional design and contrary to its own advertising, which made mention of both cab and power plant riding ahead of the front axle, Ward LaFrance actually billed the Firebrand as a *cab-over*. Boasting a turning radius of 24-feet, the Firebrand also featured the first full-width seven-man formed cab in the industry. With the motor compartment situated between the driver and officer with a rear facing bench seat, it was actually quite influential to certain, more modern engine-forward models. Though rather crude, the Firebrand was purchased

Pirsch developed its cab-forward production models off the pilot car, which was built in 1959 and later sold via Sutphen Fire Equipment to Randolph Township, Ohio. The extra large cab, which was ahead of its time, was refined into the more proportionate design. Note the vertical exhaust stack. *Steve Hagy*

Deliveries of the more refined Pirsch "Safety Cab" commenced in late 1960. Vista, California, received one of the first models in this 1000-gpm unit with 500-gallon water tank and semi-open cab. Early Pirsch cab-forwards featured headlights recessed into the cab face. By 1963, they were in protruding assemblies. *Chuck Madderom*

in bulk by several big city fire departments during its short tenure.

Two years later, Ward LaFrance introduced one of the most revered cab-forward designs of all time. The Mark I's defining characteristic was the four-piece "Ultra-Vision" windshield, which featured lower portions that angled downward, giving the

In 1960, American LaFrance amazingly introduced turbine powered fire apparatus. San Francisco received this 900 Series Turbo-Chief 1000-gpm pumper with Boeing gas turbine engine. Note the rearward facing exhaust stacks. The concept did not prove to be efficient. *Fred Crismon collection*

driver full view of the road ahead. Built of rectangular body panels, the cab measured 96-inches, the widest in the industry. Available in semi-open, canopy cab, and fully enclosed configurations, the Mark I had three versions. The P-80 was the standard cab-ahead of engine, also available in a low profile version to accommodate the Hi-Ranger articulating platforms. The P-75 (lighter GVW) and the P-85 (high end model) were of engine-forward design, with the motor compartment between the driver and officer. Ward LaFrance would also offer a more economical P-82 model, which featured the familiar TCM Cincinnati cab.

TCM was becoming more relevant as it enabled chassis providers and fire apparatus manufacturers without the means or desire to invest in the costly production of a proprietary custom cab the ability to offer one – opening the door to smaller builders and eventually allowing larger builders the opportunity to add an economical alternative to its pricier models. The softly contoured, five-man "Cincinnati Cab," as it would come to be known, would be utilized by virtually every North American manufacturer involved in *custom* fire apparatus. Most manufacturers would request or trim out slight variances in the cab to set their offerings apart. This generally consisted of prominent logos, headlight configurations, trim bands, and the style or arrangement of front air intakes/grilles. TCM would also construct exclusive cab shells to customer specifications.

The Duplex Truck Company, who dated back to 1907, was established as a specialty truck fabricator

and had been supplying big conventional chassis to several fire apparatus manufacturers. Duplex entered the cab-forward arena in conjunction with Howe Fire Apparatus. Howe was utilizing a new Duplex forward-control chassis with semi-open or canopy cab built by TCM for its custom Defender fire apparatus. Both vendors allowed Howe to market a full line of "big city" fire apparatus for "small city" budgets. This arrangement paved the way for Duplex to become a big OEM (original equipment manufacturer) player in custom cab-forward fire apparatus when it began supplying other manufacturers as well.

Additional manufacturers were jumping on the TCM bandwagon. Hahn Motors, who was infamous for producing the ungainly Spangler Dual, began offering cab-forward custom fire apparatus with Cincinnati cabs on Autocar or FWD chassis until engineering its own custom chassis in 1965. International-Harvester, who had long been content with providing commercial truck chassis to the fire service, unveiled a custom cab-forward chassis in 1963 designed expressly for the fire service. The CO-1890 chassis was engineered by Hendrickson Mobile Equipment and also featured a Cincinnati cab.

Sutphen Fire Equipment introduced a revolutionary aerial product in 1964 that single handedly catapulted the family owned company from a regional body builder to a nationally recognized fire apparatus company. The new device was a mid-mounted telescopic boxed boom of open lattice construction with pre-piped waterway and two-man crew basket. Both 65-foot single axle and 85-foot tandem axle versions would be available on FWD, International CO-1890, and Duplex custom chassis with Cincinnati cabs from TCM.

In 1964, American LaFrance introduced the Pioneer I with the purpose of offering an economical custom alternative to its high end 900 Series. Made exclusively for American LaFrance by TCM, it featured a "control tower" five-man canopy cab constructed entirely of flat sheet metal panels. Its defining characteristic was a large one-piece windshield with triangular side windows that angled forward. The Pioneer I would be available for both pumpers and aerials.

Young Fire Equipment introduced one of the most distinctive cab-forward models ever produced in 1967. The dramatically styled Crusader was designed by Richard E. Young. Yet again influenced by bus design, the low profile 94-inch wide cab with huge wraparound windshield was placed on a special chassis from the Madsen Company with indented frame. The Crusader featured raised tunnel assemblies on each side of the cab roof, which contained forward warning flashers and rearward periscope-style mirrors.

In 1967, Mack replaced the popular C-Series with the CF-Series as its lone offering exclusive to the fire service. The CF was unique in that it was purchased by small volunteer departments on up to the largest municipal departments, making it one of the most popular custom cab-forward fire chassis ever built. The powerful CF was among the first to be primarily powered by diesel engines and continued Mack's tradition of being the only fire apparatus manufacturer to produce and use its own powertrain components. It also accommodated the Aerialscope platform, which Mack had introduced in 1964 on the C-Series chassis.

Seagrave, who had been acquired by FWD, introduced the Rear Admiral aerial ladders in 1967, coinciding with production of a low-profile 80-inch wide cab, which became the Seagrave "S" model. This style established the concept of low-profile cab-forward chassis for aerial apparatus, with obvious benefits, which would be duplicated by many other manufacturers. The Seagrave Rear Admirals also pioneered the modern use of rear-steering axles, which further improved maneuverability. Seagrave replaced their original cab-forward in 1969 with the updated 80-inch wide P model. By now Seagrave had essentially taken over production of fire apparatus in Clintonville as FWD had diverted its attention to specialty trucks. However, the FWD nameplate would continue to appear on certain fire apparatus, especially those equipped with four-wheel-drive.

The Oshkosh Truck Corporation had long been noted for its all-wheel-drive specialty trucks and eventually became an ARFF apparatus giant. In 1969, Oshkosh introduced the A-Series low-profile cab-forward fire apparatus chassis with TCM cab. It was most prevalent for aerial apparatus and commonly associated with Snorkels. Pierce Manufacturing was an up and coming fire apparatus manufacturer most noted for its early commercial truck bodies and recent work as a primary body builder for Pitman Snorkel. Pierce also unveiled its new Fire Marshall custom pumpers, which were initially based on the Oshkosh

A-Series chassis. Ironically, Oshkosh would acquire Pierce much later on.

American LaFrance ended the decade as a subsidiary of an industrial conglomerate. Many of the larger fire apparatus manufacturers would eventually find themselves under this type of ownership. This has proven to be the fire apparatus "deal with the devil." Immediate gratification included further product development and enhanced marketing. However, the feasts of indulgence most often culminated with being left in the gutter.

Coast Fire Apparatus offered custom cab-forward pumpers from the late 1950s into the 1960s. They are believed to have been built utilizing International-Harvester chassis and cab sheet metal. Roseburg, Oregon, operated this 1960 model with 1250-gpm pump and 400-gallon water tank. Note its usual characteristics. *Chuck Madderom*

While Los Angeles City was buying Crown pumpers in bulk, the department was going with Seagrave for aerials, including this 1960 KT 100-foot tractor-drawn with semi-open cab. Note how the non-fixed tiller kept the wheelbase relatively short. *Chuck Madderom*

Ward LaFrance introduced the Firebrand pumper in 1960. Although certainly cab-forward compared to conventional design, WLF billed it as a cab-over. Several large departments placed orders for multiple units, including Dallas, Texas. *Chuck Madderom*

Longtime truck maker Duplex entered the cab-forward arena in conjunction with Howe's line of Defender custom apparatus by providing a forward-control chassis with TCM cab. Garnerville, New York, operated this big quad with 1000-gpm pump and 500-gallon water tank. *Frank Wegloski*

Westland sold a handful of Fireliner pumpers and Snorkels in the early 1960s to Pacific Northwest departments. It is believed that Westland utilized White-Freightliner chassis and cab sheet metal. The Fireliner canopy cab featured a distinctive sloping front. Chehalis, Washington, received a matching pumper and Snorkel. *Bill Hattersley*

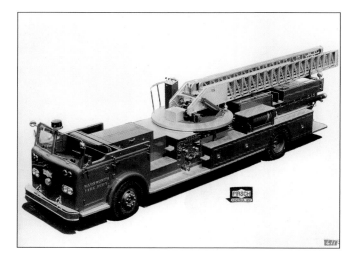

The new Pirsch cab-forward was an immediate success and available for all types of apparatus. This view of Wadsworth, Ohio's 1961 75-foot quint offers a nice view of the clean lines of the cab-forward layout. *Roger Bjorge collection*

Though declining in popularity with the advent of the quintuple combination, quads were still occasionally specified. Bedford Heights, Ohio, received this 1961 Seagrave KQ with 1000-gpm pump. *Fred Crismon collection*

In 1961, Van Pelt designed and built its own Custom 300 cab-forward model. Spring Valley, California, purchased the pilot car, which was built with a Diamond T chassis kit. The 1000-gpm unit was powered by a Waukesha 145-GZ gas engine. Subsequent units were built on Van Pelt's own frame. *Chuck Madderom*

American LaFrance introduced its Aero-Chief articulating platforms in 1962. This 900 Series served as the original demonstrator. The semi-open cab featured a windshield frame that could open to allow the 70-foot boom to lower to the dashboard so the apparatus could travel under height restrictions. *Fred Crismon collection*

The Maxim F model continued to be well received. Fort Wayne, Indiana, received this 100-foot tractor-drawn aerial with fixed tiller seat in 1962. The natural lighting and solid white paint clearly defines the distinctive characteristics of the cab. *Kent Parrish collection*

In 1962, Hahn began to offer custom cab-forward fire apparatus on either Autocar or FWD chassis with TCM Cincinnati cab. Spring Grove, Pennsylvania, operated this 1963 C-10 1000-gpm pumper with 500-gallon water tank. *Shaun P. Ryan*

Orange County, California, was a large Crown customer as well, with 42 units purchased new. The Snorkel was also a popular aerial choice on Crown chassis. Orange County operated this 1963 Firecoach with 1000-gpm pump, 300-gallon water tank, and 50-foot boom. *Chuck Madderom*

FWD cab-forward chassis was a popular choice for Snorkel apparatus. Watertown, South Dakota, received this 1963 model with bodywork by General Safety and a 65-foot boom. The FWD version of the Cincinnati cab was generally clean with no distinguishable characteristics. *Fred Crismon collection*

In 1963, International introduced its CO-1890 custom fire chassis, which was engineered by Hendrickson. It was among many models to feature the familiar TCM Cincinnati cab. International set their offering apart with a four-member grille just above the front bumper and a V-shaped emblem. This unit for Henderson, Kentucky, featured Boyer bodywork. *Fred Crismon collection*

Mack continued to develop a strong following with its exclusive C-Series fire chassis and led a surge to diesel power. Holloway Terrace, Delaware, operated this 1963 model with semi-open cab, 1000-gpm pump, and 500-gallon water tank. *Kent Parrish collection*

Seagrave was among the first manufacturers to regularly offer a four-door, fully enclosed cab-forward. Los Angeles County operated a number of units like this 1963 KB with Hall-Scott gas engine, 1250-gpm pump, and 500-gallon water tank. *Chuck Madderom*

In 1964, American LaFrance introduced the economical Pioneer I as an alternative to its pricier 900 Series. Its "control tower" cab with angled windshield was built exclusively for American LaFrance by TCM. *Walt McCall collection*

The FWD FF series was available in two-wheel-drive and all-wheel "Tractioneer" drive. Yakima County, Washington, operated this 1964 four-wheel-drive model with Western States bodywork, 750-gpm pump, and 1000-gallon water tank. *Bill Hattersley*

Los Angeles City operated many special units built by Crown. Wagon 17 ran this massive Firecoach with 2000-gpm pump, water distribution manifold system, and 400-gallon water tank. Note the busy panel and transverse hose beds. *Larry Arnold/Chuck Madderom*

Elm Grove, Illinois, operated this well-equipped 1965 C-Series with 1000-gpm pump, 250-gallon water tank, and 85-foot Pirsch mid-mounted aerial, as Mack did not make its own. Note the extended front bumper with intake and pre-connected suction made more functional by the cab-forward. *Chuck Madderom*

The Maxim F model was a very popular choice for Snorkel apparatus. Bellevue, Kentucky, received this 1965 model with 1000-gpm pump, 200-gallon water tank, and 85-foot boom. The bodywork was from Pierce, an up and coming fire apparatus manufacturer and primary body builder for the Snorkel. *Kent Parrish collection*

Ward LaFrance introduced the Mark I cab-forward in 1962 and it became an immediate success. New Orleans operated this big 1965 100-foot tractor-drawn unit with aerial by Thibault of Canada. A P-80 designation identified the high end cab-ahead of engine model. *Fred Crismon collection*

The FWD AF series was available as an aerial with several different providers. Plainville, Connecticut, received this unit in 1965 with bodywork by Farrar, a regional builder, and 85-foot mid-mount ladder from Grove. By now, protection from the elements by canopy cab was much more preferred. *Glenn Vincent*

In 1964, Mack introduced its own telescoping aerial platform, the 75-foot Aerialscope, which would become an extremely popular device, especially with New York City. Early booms were built by Truco and Eaton. Butte, Montana, operated this 1966 C-Series unit. *Bill Hattersley*

Seagrave, who had been acquired by FWD, was now essentially building all of the fire apparatus in the Clintonville complex. Catskill, New York, received this well appointed KB pumper in 1966 with 1000-gpm pump and 500-gallon water tank. *Kent Parrish collection*

The defining characteristic of the Ward LaFrance Mark I was the four-piece "Ultra-Vision" windshield, which featured lower portions that angled downward. The cab also measured 96-inches, the widest in the industry. This P-80 pumper went to Loch Sheldrake, New York, in 1966. *Fred Crismon collection*

In 1964, Sutphen introduced its revolutionary mid-mounted aerial platform which featured a telescopic boxed boom of open lattice construction with pre-piped waterway and two-man crew basket. Bethel-Tate, Ohio, operated this 1966 model on an International CO-1890 single axle chassis with TCM cab and 75-foot boom. *Jerry Sudduth*

Originally delivered to the Kingsbury Fire District in Stateline, the Nevada Division of Forestry acquired this big 1967 Firecoach equipped with Fabco four-wheel-drive and powered by a Cummins diesel engine. It had a 1500-gpm pump and 500-gallon water tank. *Chuck Madderom*

The Howe Defender on Duplex chassis was a very popular and economical fire apparatus, for small and big cities alike. Sacramento, California, received this 1250-gpm unit with 500-gallon water tank and Waukesha gas engine in 1966. The Howe name was typically prominent on the front of the cab underneath the windshield. *Chuck Madderom*

In 1967, Seagrave introduced the Rear Admiral aerials with early models featuring rear axle steering developed by FWD. Soon unveiled was a low-profile 80-inch wide cab which became the Seagrave S model, a style that would be duplicated by many manufacturers. Rear steering could be identified by the single rear tires. Chicago purchased this 100-footer. *Chuck Madderom*

Van Pelt completed a number of apparatus equipped with Hi-Ranger articulating platforms. The Florin Fire District in California operated this 85-footer on a 1967 International CO-1890 chassis with semi-open cab and V-8 gas engine. *Chuck Madderom*

Seagrave built a very functionally designed mid-mount quintuple combination. Brown Deer, Wisconsin, received this 1967 KA equipped with a 1250-gpm pump, 200-gallon water tank, and 85-foot ladder. Note the Stokes basket carried on the cab roof. *Chuck Madderom*

Oren delivered this 1000-gpm quint with 500-gallon water tank, fully compartmented body, and 65-foot Grove ladder for Camp Taylor, Kentucky, on a 1968 Duplex chassis, whose version of the Cincinnati cab was generally set apart by two low set rectangular mesh grilles just above the front bumper. *Kent Parrish*

In 1967, Mack replaced the C-Series with the flat-faced CF cab-forwards. Early versions featured a painted front with horizontal chrome strips. The CF was unique in that it was essentially a high-end model, but purchased from the smallest volunteer departments to big cities. Royersford, Pennsylvania, operated this 1968 1000-gpm model. *Shaun P. Ryan*

The Ward LaFrance S-80 was a low-profile version of the P-80, but designed especially for Hi-Ranger articulating platforms. Houghton, New York, received this big 70-foot quintuple combination on a tandem axle chassis in 1968. *Fred Crismon collection*

The Young Crusader was one of the most distinctive cab-forwards ever produced. It was built on a low profile Madsen chassis with indented frame and featured a 94-inch wide cab. Chincoteague, Virginia, received this Crusader in 1968 with a 1000-gpm pump and 1000-gallon water tank. It was later refurbished with a new generation of body. *Dennis Maag*

In 1965, Hahn began production of its own custom chassis, but still utilized the familiar Cincinnati cab. Hahn's version typically featured a wide steel band wrapping around the corners of the cab from the doors. Delaware City, Delaware, operated this 1968 C-12 with 1250-gpm pump and 1000-gallon water tank. *Shaun P. Ryan*

Crown began offering aerial apparatus in the late 1960s when Maxim ladders were made available to them. Los Angeles City received two of these 75-foot tractor-drawn aerials in 1969 with Hall-Scott gas engines. *Chuck Madderom*

Soon after its inception, the Mack CF front adopted the familiar stainless steel sheet at the front end. This 1969 model was delivered to Bellefonte, Delaware. It was equipped with a 1250-gpm pump and 500-gallon water tank. The CF continued to champion the efficiency of diesel engines started by the C-Series. *Shaun P. Ryan*

Sutphen increased the offering of its telescoping aerial platform to include an 85-foot model. The custom cab-forward chassis choices included International, FWD, and Duplex. Detroit, Michigan, purchased this unit in 1969. *Fred Crismon collection*

In 1969, Seagrave replaced the K models with a refined, 80-inch wide P model that was actually 3-inches lower. Green Haven, Maryland, operated this 1969 PB 1000-gpm pumper with 500-gallon water tank and Detroit Diesel 8V71N engine. Note how the cab-forward accommodated a wider arrangement of warning lights. *Chuck Madderom*

Specialty truck maker Oshkosh introduced its A series low-profile fire chassis with TCM cab in 1969 in conjunction with Pierce Manufacturing unveiling its custom Fire Marshall pumpers, which became popular in the Wisconsin and Chicago suburbs. *Kent Parrish collection*

Haverstraw, New York, has maintained this gorgeous 1969 Pirsch "semi" cab-forward 100-foot tractor-drawn aerial, complete with bunker gear racks common to East Coast volunteer departments of that time. *Joel Gebet*

The Hendrickson 1871-S was one of the most popular custom cab-forward chassis of the 1970s. The square cab was built exclusively for Hendrickson by TCM. Mansfield, Connecticut, operated this 1979 model with bodywork by Continental, 1000-gpm pump, and 1000-gallon water tank. *Glenn Vincent*

Chapter 4: **The 1970s**

The cab-forward concept was in full swing as the 1970s began. The Maxim S model would be the only custom conventional style to survive the decade. Traditional concepts such as semi-open cabs were nearly extinct as protection from the elements were much more preferred and standard cab width would increase to between 84 and 86 inches. The transition to diesel power continued to allow manufacturers to build even larger apparatus – from big quintuple combinations to pumper-tankers. Additional experiments with turbine powered fire apparatus by American LaFrance and Sutphen yet again failed. Fire apparatus trends of this decade greatly benefited from the cab-forward style. Aerial advances included the rear-mounted ladder and ladder-tower. A new concept that had taken hold in the Pacific Northwest had been pioneered by Western States Fire Apparatus years earlier. The "Intra-Cab" featured the fire pump

under the front of the cab with the control panel on the front face of the cab. Modern fire apparatus were also seeing more use of extended front bumpers equipped with additional warning devices, intakes, and pre-connected hand lines.

The notion that custom cab-forwards were "big city" rigs had faded as TCM was providing an avenue for just about every fire apparatus manufacturer to offer a "custom" to even the smallest of towns. TCM's business of providing generic and exclusive cab-forward shells to fire apparatus builders exploded with a new prevalence of OEM providers, allowing many newer builders to establish their custom lines and a select few to segue into the development of models of their own design and make. Duplex and Oshkosh each provided exclusive custom chassis to American Fire Apparatus, who in turn marketed their own Classic III custom chassis with TCM cabs.

In reverse, manufacturers like Van Pelt shelved their own costly custom models in favor of OEM suppliers. Commercial giants Chevrolet, Ford, and GMC even offered heavy-duty forward-control chassis for custom fire apparatus.

Many manufacturers cruised through the 1970s with slight updates. Ward LaFrance had in essence renamed its Mark I as the Ambassador under its Presidential series of custom apparatus. Young supplanted their distinctive Crusader with the more subtle Bison. Crown added a "wide-cab" version of its legendary Firecoach. Sutphen had developed its own custom chassis for pumpers and platforms. Its version of the TCM Cincinnati cab became characterized by boxed headlight and warning light bezels, now a Sutphen trait. Pirsch adopted the less costly Cincinnati cab as an alternative to its pricey Safety Cab, which received minor running changes throughout the decade. Hahn also engineered its own custom cab, the HCP, and was now building complete fire apparatus in its own plant in addition to providing its cab and chassis to other body builders.

In 1970, American LaFrance introduced a premium version of its 900 Series. The new 1000 Series featured diesel power as standard and was recognizable by a bright aluminum trim panel that wrapped around the lower front. Three years later, American LaFrance unveiled the Century Series, a completely new design. It featured an 84-inch wide cab with the canopy portion swelling out behind the front doors. To bridge the gap between the entry level Pioneer and high end Century, American LaFrance also introduced the Pacemaker series, which featured the familiar TCM Cincinnati cab. The Pioneer series saw running updates during the decade as well.

In 1970, Imperial Fire Apparatus entered the cab-forward arena. Imperial would market complete apparatus and offer its own cab-forward chassis with TCM cab in standard and low profile versions to other fire apparatus manufacturers. The Imperial name was discontinued in 1975 when its corporate parent, Pemberton Fabricators, began selling custom fire apparatus chassis under the name Pemfab. Two aptly named versions were initially offered. The first was the "84," an 84-inch wide Cincinnati-style contour cab in standard and low profile versions. The second was the radically designed "93," which was a 93-inch wide cab made exclusively for Pemfab by TCM. It featured angular wheel wells and a two-

As the 1970s began, International was still producing large numbers of its CO-1890 custom cab-forward fire chassis. Platteville, Wisconsin, received this 750-gpm quint with bodywork by American, 300-gallon water tank, and 85-foot Grove ladder. *John Javorsky/Chuck Madderom*

Van Pelt started utilizing Duplex chassis with TCM cabs as its own Custom 300 had proven to be costly to produce. The South Bay Fire District in California operated this 1250-gpm unit with 750-gallon water tank and semi-open cab. *Bill Hattersley*

piece flat windshield with face that sloped down to a protruding shelf and bumper.

In 1972, International-Harvester teamed with ally Hendrickson Mobile Equipment, an established specialty truck and component manufacturer dating back to 1913, to introduce a new cab-forward fire apparatus chassis. Initially marketed as the International FCTO, it featured an exclusive 84-inch wide square cab that was made by TCM. It was characterized by flat body panels with angular features and an inverted "U" chrome trim piece just above a chin-like

In 1970, Imperial entered the cab-forward arena by building complete fire apparatus on its own custom chassis with TCM cabs. Hometown Pemberton, New Jersey, received the first D-10 pumper. It featured a 1000-gpm pump and 500-gallon water tank. *Fred Crismon collection*

protruding front bumper. The International version was short lived as Hendrickson took ownership of the design and began marketing it as the Model 1871-S (square), commemorating the year of the Great Chicago Fire. It was complemented by the 1871-C (contour) model with low-profile options for both.

Ward LaFrance unveiled a radical new cab-forward fire apparatus in 1973. Designed and developed in conjunction with U.S. Steel, the Vantage was built on a Ford forward-control chassis with V-8 gas engine. Built as a complete unit, the Vantage featured a streamlined body with no visible compartment handles and a tilting four-door cab with "suicide" doors. Ward LaFrance again pushed the envelope in 1976 with the Patriot. It was a "low cab-forward" that sat three up front and four on a rear facing bench seat under the canopy roof. Neither design proved to be successful.

Duplex had long recognized its chassis by a myriad of alpha-numerical model numbers representing a combination of specifications. In the mid-1970s,

Duplex expanded their fire line, offering three distinct models. There were two standard height models with the R-200 having a square cab and the R-300 being a contour cab with an R-400 low-profile version. Duplex's parent company also briefly marketed its own name of Warney & Swasey rather than the Duplex brand until being sold to the Nolan Company.

In 1975, FMC developed its own custom fire apparatus cab on modified Ford L-900 chassis. This endeavor served as the catalyst to the conception of today's most prolific and innovative custom fire apparatus chassis provider. The unique FMC cab featured angular, yet boxy characteristics. After a handful had been produced, a group of former REO Truck employees approached FMC and offered to provide a custom chassis that required *no* modifications. After the deal was made and the prototype completed, Spartan Motors was born. Exclusive to FMC, the first Spartan model was the CF-1000 chassis, of which sixteen were produced. Spartan then developed the CF-2000 with contour Cincinnati cab, which was available to any manufacturer. Later versions fell under the CFA (aluminum) designation with the refined CFC contour series becoming the flagship.

Seagrave pushed the industry standard during this decade with a 92-inch wide cab, which essentially spanned the entire width, leaving no exposed steps or fenders. The low-profile "W" model was introduced in 1977 and the standard height "H" or Commander version, which became the Seagrave flagship, followed in 1979. Seagrave also incorporated removable access panels outlined with rubber zip gaskets on the face of the cab for ease of maintenance with side air intakes and extra large crew windows. In addition, Seagrave developed the "M" model, which was a no-frills economy pumper intended to compete for military contracts. It differed from other military-spec fire apparatus in that it was later offered to the civilian market.

A confusing twist towards the end of this decade involved Maxim and Ward LaFrance. Both were now owned by the same parent company and fell under the Ward LaFrance International umbrella. Pumpers would be built in the Ward LaFrance plant and aerials came out of the Maxim plant with both brands sharing the classic Ward LaFrance Ambassador cab style. The Ward LaFrance version fell under the P-87 model designation while the Maxim version was called the Maxim IV (Maxi-Vision). The original and refined F model was dubbed the Maxim II (Full-Vision). However, by 1979, due to arguable difficulties, the Ward LaFrance brand ceased, whereas Maxim survived and their custom cab-forwards came under the M (Marauder) model line.

By the end of the 1970s, Pierce had catapulted to the upper echelon of fire apparatus manufacturers. Extending from its origins as a specialty builder and building off its solid reputation for quality Snorkel bodies, Pierce had been cleverly guiding growth on its own accord. By 1979, time was ripe to develop a proprietary custom fire chassis. Purchasing the rights of an automotive legend of the same name, Pierce introduced the Arrow. Pierce smartly chose to perfect its own cab design first and relied on Duplex and Oshkosh for chassis early on. In a period when bad steel would later present quality issues for many manufacturers, Pierce was forging the use of aluminum in cab construction. It was only a matter of time before Pierce would completely take over the fire appara-

The Seagrave Rear Admiral on the low profile 80-inch wide S model chassis had proven to be a popular – from small cities on up to Chicago – and maneuverable apparatus. Ladder 24 operated this 1970 SR with 100-foot ladder. *Garry Kadzielawski*

Crown continued its relationship with Maxim for aerial ladders. Arcata, California, received this 1970 Firecoach with 100-foot ladder. The apparatus was interestingly powered by an International-Harvester V-8 gas engine with an Allison automatic transmission. *Bill Hattersley*

tus world. Another manufacturer was close behind. Rising out of sunny Florida, Emergency One had rocketed to near the top of the industry in just six years with its modular aluminum fire apparatus and was marketing custom apparatus on chassis from the likes of Hendrickson and Pemfab with delivery in as little as sixty days.

New York City has operated more Mack apparatus than any department and warmly embraced the CF model. New York City was the first department to specify as standard a four-door, fully-enclosed cab-forward. This 1971 1000-gpm CF with Thermodyne diesel was being prepared for delivery. *Fred Crismon collection*

Pirsch built some impressive apparatus on its custom cab-forward. Wood Dale, Illinois, purchased a big rescue pumper and this 1971 100-foot quint with 1000-gpm pump and 300-gallon water tank on a tandem axle chassis. *Chuck Madderom*

The distinctive Young Crusader featured raised tunnel assemblies on each side of the cab roof, which contained forward warning flashers and rearward periscope-style mirrors. Westhampton Beach, New York, received this 1971 model with 1500-gpm pump and 500-gallon water tank. *Frank Wegloski*

The semi-open cab had just about worn out its welcome in the fire service as protection from the elements was preferred. However, some departments still requested the configuration. Black Mudd, Kentucky, operated this 1000-gpm Oren pumper with 500-gallon water tank on a 1972 Duplex chassis well into the 1990s. *Kent Parrish*

Commercial providers even took advantage of the fire service transition to cab-forward chassis. GMC provided a forward-control chassis with unique TCM cab on which Pierce constructed a Fire Marshall custom 1000-gpm pumper for Pleasure Ridge Park, Kentucky. *Kent Parrish*

The Oshkosh A series fire chassis had become a dominant choice for Snorkel apparatus. Denver, Colorado, received two solid white units with red wheels on 1972 tandem axle chassis with Pierce bodywork and 85-foot booms. *Kent Parrish collection*

Custom cab-forward rescue apparatus were still quite unusual at this time. Port Jervis, New York, specified a Ward LaFrance Ambassador chassis on which Saulsbury built this walk-in heavy-duty squad with hidden 250-gpm pump and 300-gallon water tank. *Shaun P. Ryan*

The Hendrickson 1871-S was initially a joint venture with International-Harvester, who marketed the model as the FTCO (Fire Truck Cab Over). Independence Hill, Indiana, received this 1000-gpm pumper with 600-gallon water tank and Boyer bodywork in 1972. *Chuck Madderom*

Ward LaFrance introduced the radical Vantage fire apparatus in 1973 which featured a streamlined body and tilting four-door cab with "suicide" front doors on a modified Ford chassis. California City purchased this 1000-gpm demonstrator unit with 500-gallon water tank. *Chuck Madderom*

Young introduced the more subtle Bison apparatus, which featured a low-profile TCM cab on chassis from Madsen or Walter. Cherry Hill, New Jersey, received this 1500-gpm unit with 500-gallon water tank and popular 50-foot Tele-Squrt aerial device. *Kent Parrish collection*

American LaFrance added a moderately priced model to bridge the gap between the Pioneer I and premium models. The Pacemaker featured the familiar TCM Cincinnati cab. It was available for pumpers and aerials of all types. Los Angeles County operated this 1973 100-foot Ladder Chief. *Chuck Madderom*

Mack's popular Aerialscope platform was now based on the CF series. It was requested by departments big and small. Lyndon, Kentucky, received this unit in 1973 with 75-foot boom that was now being supplied by Baker. *Kent Parrish collection*

Though nearly extinct, a handful of semi-open custom cab-forwards would be produced into the early 1980s. Delanco, New Jersey, operated this beautiful 1973 Seagrave PB 1000-gpm pumper with 350-gallon water tank and extended front bumper with a tray for the pre-connected suction line. *Scott Mattson*

The Mack CF was also a popular choice of chassis for the Snorkel product line with Pierce bodies. This included the articulating platforms, the Squrt and the Tele-Squrt. Eunice in Louisiana, a strong Mack sales territory, received this 50-foot boom on a 1973 CF chassis. *Kent Parrish collection*

By the early 1970s, Sutphen had developed its own custom chassis. Their version of the TCM Cincinnati cab featured boxed headlight and warning light bezels that became a Sutphen trademark. Northbrook, Illinois, operated this 1973 unit with 1000-gpm pump, 350-gallon water tank, and 85-foot tower. *Leo Duliba*

Ward LaFrance offered a 4x4 version of the Ambassador that featured angled front wheel wells, typically for ARFF apparatus. Rugged San Bernardino County, California, maintained this 1973 municipal model with 1500-gpm pump and 500-gallon water tank. *Garry Kadzielawski*

Though known mostly for its aerial platforms, Sutphen had also begun churning out quality custom pumpers. Rocky Point, New York, received this 1500-gpm unit with 500-gallon water tank in 1974. Note the additional seating forward of the pump panel. *John Toomey*

American LaFrance had started offering a premium version of its 900 Series in 1972. The new 1000 Series featured an aluminum chrome wraparound band and stainless steel pump panel. Cottage Grove, Oregon, operated this big 1974 2000-gpm pumper-tanker with 1500-gallon water tank. *Bill Hattersley*

In addition to the premium 1000 Series, American LaFrance unveiled an updated Pioneer II, which was essentially a more dressed up version with additional lower front trim. Galt, California, received this 1250-gpm unit with 500-gallon water tank and 50-foot Tele-Squrt in 1974. *Chuck Madderom*

American Fire Apparatus offered custom apparatus on disguised Duplex cab-forward chassis with TCM cabs. The tower ladder concept was also rapidly gaining favor. Fairfax City, Virginia, operated this 1974 model with 85-foot Grove tower ladder. *Shaun P. Ryan*

The Calavar Firebird was the tallest aerial apparatus in the United States. Many quickly found new homes after proving to be too big for their original owners. Sacramento, California, received this 150-footer via Anchorage, Alaska, on a low profile 1974 Hendrickson 1871-LPS chassis. *Chuck Madderom*

Duplex continued to offer cab-forward chassis under a myriad of alpha-numerical model numbers that represented a combination of chassis configuration and engines, among other specifications. Riverside, California, operated this 1974 Howe Defender with 1000-gpm pump, 500-gallon water tank, 80-gallon foam cell, and roof turret. *Chuck Madderom*

Western States pioneered the "intra-cab" configuration in which the pump sat under the front seat with the panel being on the face of the cab. FWD/Seagrave generally provided the bulk of chassis under a friendly arrangement with Western States. Jackson County, Oregon, received this 1250-gpm unit with 2000-gallon water tank in 1974 on a Seagrave PC ("C" for chassis only). *Chuck Madderom*

In the mid 1970s, Duplex expanded its fire chassis lineup with three distinct models. The new R-200 was characterized by its square cab, flat front, single-piece windshield, and tear drop quarter windows. Vallejo, California, operated this 1974 Howe Defender with 1250-gpm pump and 750-gallon water tank. *Bill Hattersley*

The Ward LaFrance Ambassador continued to be a very popular custom model. Serena, Illinois, received this rig in 1974. Serving as a tanker, it was equipped with a 1000-gpm pump and 750-gallon water tank. A folding dump tank slid in the body from the rear, where upper compartments would normally be. *Don Feipel*

In the mid 1970s, Pirsch updated its custom cab-forward with 3/4 "barrier" style doors, namely to reduce costs in sheet metal over full length doors. Louisville, Kentucky, was a strong Pirsch customer. The department received two of these 1000-gpm pumpers with 300-gallon water tanks in 1974. *Kent Parrish collection*

In 1973, American LaFrance unveiled the completely new Century Series. It featured an 84-inch wide cab and rear canopy portion that swelled out past the front doors with side air intakes. Westminster, Maryland, purchased this 1975 model with 1000-gpm pump and 1000-gallon water tank. *Jeff Mogush*

The R-400 was Duplex's new low-profile offering. It was very similar to the versions with TCM cabs offered by the likes of Oshkosh and others. Sharon, Connecticut, operated this 85-foot LTI tower ladder with Oren bodywork on a 1974 chassis. Note the stubby rear. *Mark Redman*

FWD/Seagrave fire apparatus had in essence become the same. The FWD name generally appeared only on specialty apparatus. This 50-foot Snorkel with 1250-gpm pump and 350-gallon water tank for Winnetka, Illinois, was no exception. It was built on a 1975 P model four-wheel-drive chassis with four-door cab and rear-steering. *Chuck Madderom*

Hahn was now building its own custom cab-forward model, the HCP, which was built entirely in its plant and featured an attractive 84-inch wide cab. Shaker Pines, Connecticut, received this 1500-gpm pumper with 1000-gallon water tank in 1975. *Glenn Vincent*

The American LaFrance Pioneer III featured a wider "control tower" cab with a shelf below the windshield and horizontal light bezels backed by vinyl. Also offered was a more economic version built on a Chevrolet chassis with V-8 gas engine, called the Spartan/1. Santa Barbara, California, operated this 1976 Pioneer III with 1000-gpm pump and 500-gallon water tank. *Chuck Madderom*

In 1977, Crown supplemented the venerable, but dated Firecoach with a "wide-cab" version. Rubidoux, California, received the first unit. Powered by a Cummins NTF-295 diesel engine, it was equipped with a 1250-gpm pump and 500-gallon water tank. *Chuck Madderom*

In addition to the popular 1871-S, Hendrickson offered a version with contour cab – the 1871-C. Clark was a popular, regional builder who offered custom models on Hendrickson chassis. San Diego, California, operated this 1250-gpm unit with 500-gallon water tank on a 1976 chassis. *Chuck Madderom*

The new Pemfab, who had evolved from Imperial, offered custom fire apparatus chassis to practically any builder. Irvington, Nebraska, received this 85-foot LTI tower ladder with private label Conestoga bodywork and 1976 Pemfab "84" low profile chassis. *Chuck Madderom*

Wade Hampton, North Carolina, operated this 1976 Pirsch custom 1000-gpm quint with 75-foot mid-mount ladder, a configuration whose popularity was starting to fade. Note the small port windows between the front door and standard location for the canopy cab windows. *Fred Crismon collection*

Cincinnati, Ohio, had Seagrave build fully enclosed "riot-proof" fire apparatus based on the P model chassis. Lawrenceburg, Indiana, "piggy-backed" on the pumper order in 1976 with this 1500-gpm unit with 750-gallon water tank. The fully enclosed body featured a removable diamond plate panel for engine and pump access. *Steve Hagy*

The venerable Mack CF continued to be one of best selling cab-forward fire trucks in the fire service. Homewood, Illinois, received this 1250-gpm model with 750-gallon water tank with high side compartments, which was quickly becoming more popular. *Garry Kadzielawski*

In 1975, FMC began building a unique custom cab on a modified Ford L-900 chassis. A group of former REO employees offered FMC a custom chassis that required no modifications, resulting in the first Spartan Motors fire chassis, the CF-1000 (and later CFA-1000), which was exclusive to FMC, an example being this 1977 model for Cortland, Illinois. Sixteen Spartan/FMC combinations were produced. *Dennis J. Maag*

American Fire Apparatus was marketing its own Classic III custom models, based on Oshkosh low-profile and Duplex standard height chassis. Sunnyslope, Washington, received this rig in 1977 with 1500-gpm pump and 200-gallon water tank. It featured American's 65-foot Aqua Jet telescopic waterway and rack loaded with ground ladders. *Bill Hattersley*

The second fire chassis offered by Spartan was the CF-2000, which soon became the CFA-2000, and generally featured FTI bodywork. The earlier version featured square automotive headlights that were actually purchased from Cadillac. Moraine, Ohio, operated this 1977 model with 1000-gpm pump and 1000-gallon water tank. *Shaun P. Ryan*

Hendrickson was also offering a low-profile version of its contour cab. St. Louis, Missouri, operated this 85-foot Snorkel with Pierce bodywork on a 1977 1871-LPC chassis. Hendrickson still utilized the boxy bumper and headlight assembly for its contour models. *Dennis J. Maag*

The Spartan contour cab went through several refinements before eventually becoming the CFC series. A 2000 suffix designated two axles, while a 3000 indicated three. The Boles Fire District in Missouri received this rig in 1977 with 1250-gpm pump, 750-gallon water tank, and FMC bodywork. *Dennis J. Maag*

Sturgis, Michigan, operated one of the more unusual aerials on a Mack CF chassis. This 1977 model featured a 1000-gpm front-mounted pump and 250-gallon water tank. Thibault provided the 85-foot aerial and Hamerly completed the bodywork. *Garry Kadzielawski*

Though Oshkosh was already noted for its low-profile chassis, it went even lower, nearly to the ground, for its new L series, generally utilized for aerial apparatus. Menasha, Wisconsin, received this sleek rig with 100-foot LTI ladder and Pierce bodywork in 1977. *John Javorsky/Chuck Madderom*

The Pemfab "93" or "Wedge" cab was made exclusively for Pemfab by TCM. It featured angular wheel wells and a two-piece flat windshield and face that sloped down to a shelf just above the protruding front bumper. New Lenox, Illinois, operated this 1977 model with LTI 100-foot rear-mount aerial ladder. *Garry Kadzielawski*

The P-82 was Ward LaFrance's economical custom featuring the familiar TCM Cincinnati cab. Dallas, Texas, Engine 6 ran with this 1977 model with 1000-gpm pump and 500-gallon water tank. Note the Ward LaFrance style grille above the front bumper. *Chuck Madderom*

Maxim and WLF were now both owned by the same parent company and fell under the Ward LaFrance International umbrella with pumpers being built in the Ward LaFrance plant. In addition to sharing the Ambassador styled cab, Maxim continued to market its original F model. Coventry, Rhode Island, received this 1750-gpm foam pumper with 500-gallon water tank and 110-foam cell in 1978. *Shaun P. Ryan*

The "84" was Pemfab's standard fire service offering. Baltimore County, Maryland operated this 1250-gpm unit with 500-gallon water tank, 55-foot Readi-Tower, and Grumman-Oren bodywork. It featured a fully enclosed cab with 3/4 doors and diamond plate lowers. Note the position of the middle crew window. *Joel Woods*

Pirsch was beginning to struggle with delivery times and costs due to the timely and expensive construction of its custom "Safety Cab." So, it also adopted the TCM Cincinnati cab. Their version became extremely popular and kept Pirsch in the playing field. Bartlett, Tennessee, received this 1000-gpm pumper in 1978. *Fred Crismon collection*

Military spec fire apparatus were generally kept to the confines of bases and designed solely for the branches; therefore, not indicative of general fire apparatus evolution. However, the slab sided Seagrave M model, such as this 1978 Naval unit, was unique in that it was later adapted and marketed for the civilian market. *Garry Kadzielawski*

In its later years Ward LaFrance used aerials from its sister company Maxim. The Ambassador styled cab now fell under the P-87 model designation and could also be badged as a Maxim. New Albany, Indiana, purchased two of these 1978 models with 100-foot rear-mounted ladders. *Jerry Sudduth*

Ward LaFrance again pushed the envelope in 1976 with the radically designed Patriot. It was a "low cab-forward" that sat three up front and four on a rear facing bench set under the canopy roof. Thornton, Colorado, operated this 1978 model with 1000-gpm pump and 500-gallon water tank. However, the legendary Ward LaFrance name would not survive past 1978. *Shaun P. Ryan*

The R-300 was now Duplex's standard fire chassis with contoured Cincinnati cab. Thomaston, Connecticut, received this rig in 1979 with 1500-gpm pump, 1000-gallon water tank, and Oren-Grumman bodywork. Canopy cabs soon started being retrofitted with flip-up "Man Saver" bars as a safety measure to help prevent firefighters from falling from the jump seat area. *Kent Parrish collection*

Hahn had become a predominantly "custom" manufacturer, producing its own models and offering chassis to other builders such as Clark, JACO, LTI/Conestoga, and Saulsbury. Glastonbury, Connecticut, ran this 1979 HCP with 1000-gpm pump and 750-gallon water tank. *Glenn Vincent*

Specialty truck manufacturer Hendrickson also offered 4x4 fire apparatus chassis. Ishpeming Township, Michigan, specified this top-mount 750-gpm pumper with 750-gallon water tank with Pierce bodywork on a 1979 1871-S 4x4 chassis. *Garry Kadzielawski*

The Pirsch custom with Cincinnati cab was now dominating the production line in Kenosha. Their version often featured boxed headlights to set it apart from others. The hometown department received this 100-foot rear-mount ladder in 1979. *Kent Parrish collection*

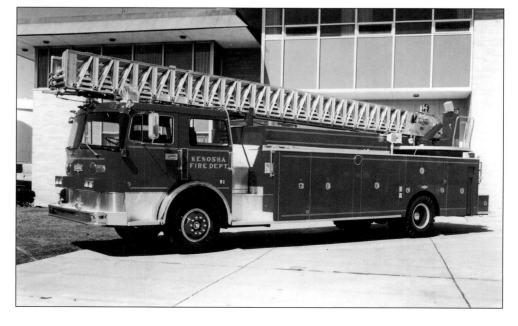

The standard Spartan fire chassis with contour cab was now called the CFC series. This pumper with Boyer bodywork served as a demonstrator model. The cab of the refined CFC series generally featured a stainless steel wraparound band with dual headlights and turn signals combined into square, protruding housings. *Kent Parrish collection*

In 1977, Seagrave introduced an additional low-profile offering, the W model, which was regularly used for pumpers. It featured a wider, 92-inch cab with removable front access panels outlined with rubber zip gaskets and side air intakes. St. Peters, Missouri, operated this 1979 model with 1000-gpm pump and 750-gallon water tank. *Dennis J. Maag*

In 1979, Seagrave introduced the H model, a standard height version of the W model, which became their flagship cab for the next decade. Fairfax County, Virginia, received this 100-foot tractor-drawn aerial in 1979. It even featured a training seat on the exterior of the tiller cab. *Mike Sanders*

In 1979, Pierce stormed the market with the first custom cab offering of its own make and design. Pierce chose to utilize an already established Oshkosh V series chassis on which to first perfect its new Arrow cab. Pierce also pioneered aluminum cab construction and revolutionized fire apparatus cab design. Early Arrows featured boxy dual headlight assemblies. *Shaun P. Ryan*

In 1984, after rocketing to the top of the industry in just ten years, the relatively new Emergency-One introduced its own custom chassis with wide, square cab – the Hurricane. The Kennedy Space Center in Florida operated this 1984 model with 1250-gpm pump, 300-gallon water tank, and 95-foot ladder tower. *Garry Kadzielawski*

Chapter 5: **The 1980s**

The video music era began with the first Music Television (MTV) video "Video Killed the Radio Star," a relevant analogy for how progressive *and* aggressive fire apparatus manufacturers, namely Pierce and Emergency One, became all the rage and stormed the charts, leaving aging legends in the nostalgic past. The new stars began dominating the market with multiple custom models in every price range. As the "next generation" flourished, many of the great names in fire apparatus struggled to keep up with the explosive progression.

The 1980s saw a dilution of the *cab-forward* term. Many manufacturers began to embrace the tilt-cab concept. Simultaneously, engines and power trains

became more efficient. These factors resulted in the motor compartment encroaching further into the front portion of the cab, presenting a more modern *engine-forward* delineation. This period also saw the advent of revolutionary mid and rear-engine designs. Cab width continued to increase as well with some models reaching 96 inches. Once a limited option, fully enclosed cabs with spacious interiors and creature comforts such as air-conditioning became more common. Cab construction also continued to evolve with the use of aluminum and stainless steel. Diesel had become the sole motive power in this segment with Caterpillar, Cummins, and Detroit Diesel dominating an industry once led by gasoline giants

Hall-Scott and Waukesha. Manual transmissions were also fading into history with Allison automatics forming a monopoly.

The new fire apparatus studs began to spin wheelies around the legends, most of who labored through the decade. American LaFrance continued to bank on its Century Series and the Straightline version had become the sole economy model. In 1985 the industry was stunned when new corporate parent Figgie International shut the division down. However, a year later, American LaFrance was reborn with Kersey Manufacturing, who introduced an all new Century 2000 cab as well as reviving the Pacemaker program, both of which utilized Pemfab chassis.

In 1982, Young introduced the innovative Crusader II, which featured a mid-engine design. The fire pump was mounted under the front of the cab with hydraulically controlled valves. It was built on a Duplex chassis with the forward portion of the cab being a D-350 style and the unique option of side-entry bus style crew doors. Hahn introduced its new "92" model in 1983 with an engine-forward HCTP split-tilt cab version coming five years later. Despite a healthy backlog, amid a heavy debt load and other internal issues, Hahn was forced to close its doors in 1989.

In 1984, Mack made the surprise announcement that it would cease the production of complete fire apparatus, but continue to make available its venerable CF cab-forward fire chassis for any manufacturer to place its own body on, which many of the newer builders readily took advantage of. Emergency One even published a detailed memo to its dealers with instructions on how to capitalize.

Maxim and Pirsch were the last two fire apparatus manufacturers to cease production of their long-nosed conventional models with Maxim continuing to offer its S model until the very end. Both were also in dire straits. Despite resuscitation efforts and a revamped F model with TCM cab on Pemfab chassis, Maxim shut down for good in 1989. Pirsch was suffering from extended delivery times and a lawsuit over a firefighter ironically falling from a "Safety Cab" in addition to rising production costs. This resulted in the last of its classic cab-forwards being delivered in 1982 and a newly designed cab in conjunction with TCM.

Duplex entered the decade with the full width D-250 square cab, which evolved into the D-260.

The 84-inch wide Spartan CFC with updated front trim/headlight assembly was now being utilized by most every manufacturer that built "custom" fire apparatus. Car-Mar constructed this massive 1000-gpm unit with 3000-gallon water tank on a 1980 chassis for Summit Station, Pennsylvania. *Shaun P. Ryan*

Duplex added the D-250 to its lineup, in following with the trend towards wider cabs that extended flush over the wheel wells with more windshield glass. The D-250 featured a flat front with sloped windshield, front "brow", and vertical quarter windows. Hayward, California, operated this 1250-gpm pumper with 500-gallon water tank and Howe-Grumman bodywork. *Chuck Madderom*

Both styles featured flat windshields and quarter windows. The D-350 Enforcer had become the standard contour cab offering with the D-450 being the low-profile version. Each featured soft lines and a standard, but generally pleasing appearance. In 1987, Simon, a European company, purchased Duplex, who introduced the new D-500 Vanguard chassis, which featured a split-tilt cab and offered a multitude of options.

Upstart Emergency-One heavily favored the Pemfab chassis and "84" cab for its "custom" apparatus. Riverside, California, received this aerial in 1981 with 106-foot Hahn Fire Spire rear-mount ladder, which was made available to Emergency-One as it developed its own aerial. *Chuck Madderom*

Though still relatively new, Spartan quickly surpassed the Duplex chassis lineup. The 84-inch wide CFV Maxi-Vision combined both contour and square attributes with a substantial windshield with a 92-inch CFH version soon following. The early Spartan flagship was the CFC series, which would evolve and mutate into two 94-inch wide versions. The CFG "Spacemaster" featured a flat windshield and front while the CFC "Supercab" maintained contour characteristics. Spartan offered "ready" cabs in galvanneal or stainless steel, or aluminum – already painted to match and trimmed to specifications. Spartan also strayed from the monopoly of TCM by contracting with Marion Body Works, who began building its exclusive cab shells by 1990.

In 1983, Spartan introduced the venerable Gladiator version of its CFG chassis. The initial style was of engine-forward design with motor access via a hinged cover between the driver and officer or by a subframe that slid out from behind the front grille. A full tilt configuration was offered later in the decade. In addition to the standard canopy cab, the Gladiator was available as a fully enclosed "Super Command Cab" version with 20-inch raised roof. The forerunner of many of today's designs, among the advantages

of this concept was standing room, multi-purpose functions, and enclosed top-mount pump panels.

Spartan would eventually identify its chassis with a full code number that indicated the specifications of the chassis in addition to a marketable model name. The standard fixed cab was called the Monarch. The innovative "Eurospace" style featured a fully enclosed cab interior that was completely open with no partition between the front and rear. Spartan also introduced their versions of mid and rear-mount engine models in the Baron and Silent Knight, respectively.

Pemfab was also quietly accumulating an equally impressive array of custom fire chassis with a lineup identified by descriptive model numbers as well as marketable names. The standard fixed cab had become the Royale with a low-profile Sovereign version. The "93" cab became the Wedge, then the Premiere. However, the flagship would be the new Imperial tilt-cab, which featured an expansive option list. Pemfab also provided two unique agendas which greatly benefited other manufacturers. The Monogram program essentially gave a customer or manufacturer the ability to dream up any combination of cab and chassis style which could be customized as their own marketable model, with examples being

Gator and FMC. The Marquis was a stripped chassis available for any manufacturer to place its own cab on. It was utilized by Kersey/American LaFrance for the Century 2000 and by Maxim for its late F model.

Hendrickson remained a relevant OEM provider for the first half of the decade. The original 1871-S was updated to the 95-inch wide 1871-W and the contour version was widened to the 94-inch 1871-CS. In 1985, Hendrickson introduced a WT (tilt-cab) version of the 1871. Shortly thereafter, the fire line was sold to upstart Kovatch Mobile Equipment (KME), who continued the 1871 styles under its own model names. The Firehawk was based off the fixed cab 1871-W. The Firefox was essentially the 1871-CS and the 1871-WT was named the Renegade.

By 1983, Pierce had engineered its own custom fire chassis and simultaneously introduced its second custom, the Dash, which was partly based on the Fleet Arrow, of its Utility line. Depending on engine choice, the Dash was available in cab or engine-forward configuration with canopy cab as standard and optional two-door sedan cab. Two years later, Pierce unveiled the high end engine-forward Lance, which enabled relevancy in multi-purpose cab configurations with fully enclosed and raised roof options. Pierce had become the undisputed industry giant and even went after the commercial market. A D-8000 version of the Dash directly targeted the popular Ford C-8000 with a Caterpillar 3208-T diesel engine and similar components, but in a competitively priced custom package. Pierce finished the decade by offering another revolutionary concept. The Javelin featured a rear-mounted engine and front wheel drive with open cab interior. The cab, chassis, and body were built together and the water tank was situated between the cab and pump.

Upstart Emergency One, who had shot to the top of the industry in just ten years, introduced the aptly named Hurricane, its first of three rapid fire offerings, in 1984. It was characterized by a low set, wide cab with huge windshield. Emergency One's parent company, Federal Signal, also formed Federal Motors, who would be tasked with building its custom fire chassis in addition to specialty products. Just a year later, the revolutionary Hush custom fire chassis was introduced. It featured a rear-mounted engine and fully-enclosed cab. Gone was the engine doghouse in the cab, which resulted in a spacious and quiet interior

Although the old P model design was still available, the new H model had become the preferred Seagrave offering. Centreville, Maryland, purchased this 1981 model with 1000-gpm pump and 750-gallon water tank. The H model design featured very roomy jump seats with a great deal of window area. *Leo Duliba*

In 1981, after increasing costs and production times, Pirsch delivered the last of its own custom Cab-Forward design to Bloomington, Illinois. It was equipped with a 1250-gpm pump and 750-gallon water tank. Unfortunately and ironically, the "Safety Cab" would be called into question in a later lawsuit involving a firefighter death. *Chuck Madderom*

for the crew. Sequentially and now known simply as "E-One" the Cyclone was introduced in 1986. This cab-forward was characterized by a slightly higher set cab with more contour features.

Seagrave skated through the decade relatively unscathed. The M model military-spec pumper was released to the civilian market as the Invader. The low-profile W model was replaced with the L, a four-door model with staggered lines, in 1989. The flagship H model thrived until it was supplanted by a completely redesigned Commander, the J model, in

Duplex continued to offer the contoured D-300, in both two and three axle versions, during the early 1980s. Bolton, Connecticut, operated this clean looking 1000-gpm unit with 2000-gallon water tank and Oren-Grumman bodywork on a 1981 chassis. *Leo Duliba*

1988. Family owned Sutphen continued to thrive in its niche as a regional manufacturer and off its famous aerial platforms. The company continued to eschew marketable model names until the "Deluge" moniker came about for its pumpers. TCM had also helped develop a refined cab more in line with industry standards, but still with the characteristic boxed light assemblies Sutphen had become known for.

Kidron was another longtime specialty truck manufacturer who broke into the fire business when it was contracted by Ladder Towers Inc. (LTI) to build an exclusive custom cab called the Olympian, which was placed on a Duplex L series chassis and marketed as a complete aerial unit in addition to serving as an avenue for LTI to enter the pumper market. Ottawa Truck was a Kansas-based specialty truck manufacturer. From the mid 1980s into the early 1990s it offered a 94-inch wide custom cab-forward fire apparatus chassis. It was available to several body builders, but was used extensively and marketed by Beck Fire Apparatus. An engine-forward tilt-cab model would follow before Ottawa exited the fire business.

By 1988, Grumman, who had become one of the largest fire apparatus manufacturers, decided the time was right to experiment with the development of its own custom chassis. First came the low profile Panther I chassis for its Aerialcat line with an exclusive cab made by TCM. Following was a standard height Panther II pumper chassis on which Grumman built its own cab shell. Quickly deciding against the costs of further engineering and production, Grumman contracted with specialty truck maker HME, who had become established off certain assets sold by Hendrickson. HME provided the chassis for both the Aerialcats and pumpers with TCM building the cab shells. After a trial period of having Spartan finish the cabs, HME was contracted for cab completion as well. This arrangement gave Grumman exclusive proprietary designs while setting up HME for later entry into the fire business. Depending on availability, Grumman also continued to use the Duplex D-450 chassis and Duplex-trimmed cabs for the Aerialcats if necessary or requested.

As the decade came to end, the pioneers of cab-forward fire apparatus had become irrelevant and the end had come or was near for most of the classic names. Arguably the most innovative decade in the history of fire apparatus, a new generation of progressive manufacturers had begun refining the original concepts into the modern machines of today.

In the late 1970s and into the early 1980s, Spartan offered the CFV and CFH series, which featured an 84-inch and later 92-inch wide cab that combined flat and contoured cab attributes with "Maxi-Vision" windshield. The Chesterfield Fire Protection District in Missouri received this 1250-gpm unit with 400-gallon water tank, 55-foot Readi-Tower, and FMC bodywork on a 1981 CFV chassis. *Dennis J. Maag*

Western States maintained its relationship with Seagrave and continued to favor its custom chassis for Intra-Cab apparatus. Beaverton, Oregon, received this unit on a 1981 HC chassis with 1250-gpm pump and 1000-gallon water tank. Note the busy appearance of the front of the cab and black vinyl lowers. *Chuck Madderom*

American LaFrance essentially replaced the Pioneer and Pacemaker series with the economy Century II model, which was also called the Straightline and Spartan II. It featured an exclusive TCM-built cab with less costly flat body panels and a single-piece windshield. National City, California, operated this 1982 model with 1500-gpm pump and 500-gallon water tank. *Chuck Madderom*

Hendrickson had updated its chassis offerings to include the 1871-W, which was lower profile than the 1871-S and featured a wider cab that extended flush with the wheel wells, which were angular. Emergency-One favored this chassis for its new, exclusive aerials. Tyler, Texas, operated this 1982 110-foot aerial ladder. *Eric Hansen*

American LaFrance began to lose steam in the 1980s as upstarts had taken over the industry and aluminum construction was becoming more favored. Lemont, Illinois, received this Century pumper with four-door cab, 1500-gpm pump, and 500-gallon water tank in 1982. *Garry Kadzielawski*

American LaFrance had introduced a "low-boy" version of its Century chassis, which was primarily used for its aerial line. Wheatridge, Colorado, operated this 1500-gpm Water Chief quint with 250-gallon water tank and 100-foot ladder. *Shaun P. Ryan*

Continental, a popular East Coast regional builder, introduced its own custom model in 1980. The Compac was based on International power train components and bolted front-end sheet metal for the unique cab design. Essex, Massachusetts, purchased the pilot car with 1250-gpm pump and 500-gallon water tank. *Shaun P. Ryan*

Montvale, New Jersey, is known for being the THE East Coast department to operate Crown Firecoaches — in fact, four of them, including this 1983 wide-cab version with 1500-gpm pump and 500-gallon water tank. After closing and being revived in a deal with Van Pelt/FMC, the last Crown Firecoach was built in 1985, ending the run of a legendary and revolutionary cab-forward chassis. *Joel Gebet*

The CFL series was Spartan's low profile offering. As typical, it was generally reserved for aerial apparatus. The early version featured a contour cab, while a later version had a wider cab, nearly identical to others such as Duplex's offering. North Pole, Alaska, received this 75-foot Tele-Squrt with 1500-gpm pump, 300-gallon water tank, and Emergency-One bodywork in 1983. *Garry Kadzielawski*

The original Hendrickson 1871-S was losing steam, but still offered into the early 1980s. This nice looking unit with 1500-gpm pump and 2000-gallon water tank featured Continental bodywork. It was built in 1983 for Vernon, Connecticut. *Glenn Vincent*

Cromwell, Connecticut, operated this 75-foot Aerialscope on a tandem axle Mack CF chassis. It was among the first such units to be equipped as a quintuple combination. The 1983 model featured a 1500-gpm pump and 300-gallon water tank. *Mark Redman*

Hendrickson continued to refine its fire chassis lineup with the wide, contoured 1871-CS. This functional style of cab would become the industry norm for the rest of the decade. B & S Fire completed the bodywork on this 1000-gpm pumper with 750-gallon water tank in 1983 for the Grand Canyon National Park. *Garry Kadzielawski*

While Ward LaFrance did not survive the 1970s, its sister company, Maxim, did. Maxim began marketing its cab-forwards under the M (Marauder) lineup. The hold-over model was the Maxim II - Full-Vision styled cab, such as this 85-foot mid-mount ladder delivered to Holliston, Massachusetts, in 1983. *Shaun P. Ryan*

By 1983, after using Oshkosh and Duplex chassis, Pierce had settled on the Arrow cab design, had developed its own custom fire chassis and was now building complete custom apparatus from the ground up in its own facilities. The updated Arrow could be distinguished by the more rounded headlight bezels. Charles County, Maryland, operated this 1983 model. *Shaun P. Ryan*

Pemfab greatly expanded its fire chassis lineup in the 1980s, including the low profile Sovereign model. Pirsch, who had discontinued its own custom cab, was now relying completely on others. This 110-foot Sky Top aerial was delivered to Catskill, New York, in 1983. *Ron Bogardus*

Duplex had refined the D-250 and renamed it the D-260, which retained some of the original characteristics, but with less sharp lines. Walter completed the bodywork on this 1000-gpm pumper with 750-gallon water tank and 100-gallon foam cell for the Veterans Affairs Hospital in Coatesville, Pennsylvania. *Dennis J. Maag*

Spartan also continued to greatly expand its fire chassis lineup, including the enlarged 94-inch wide CFC "Supercab" contour series. This general width had also become the industry norm. North Montgomery County, Texas, received this big 1000-gpm unit with 2000-gallon water tank and Emergency-One bodywork in 1984. *Glenn Vincent*

Cedarburg, Wisconsin, operated this 1984 Seagrave HB 1500-gpm pumper with 750-gallon water tank. Equipped with four-wheel-drive, it also received an FWD nameplate. The rig is believed to have been the first fully enclosed "fixed-cab" fire apparatus with a raised roof. *Chuck Madderom*

The Spartan CFG "Spacemaster" could be distinguished by the slight lip separating the front and windshield of the flat cab. It was the lower cost alternative to the CFC series. Spartan was also one of the few cab/chassis providers that would accommodate an Intra-Cab configuration. Washington County, Oregon, received this 1250-gpm unit with 1000-gallon water tank and Western States bodywork. *Chuck Madderom*

The Spartan CFG series also consisted of the high end "Gladiator" version, which featured a forward mounted engine, allowing for more room in the crew area. It was also available in fully enclosed "Command Cab" versions with "Super Command Cab" raised roof options. Among the first was this heavy rescue with Frontline bodywork on a 1984 chassis for North Palos, Illinois. *Garry Kadzielawski*

Duplex also continued to expand its fire chassis lineup. The D-450 (with "T" suffix for tandem) Defender was the new low profile offering, which featured a much wider cab than the previous D-400. It was the preferred choice for Grumman's new Aerialcat ladder tower. Fresno, California, received this 1985 102-foot model. *Chuck Madderom*

In 1983, Hahn introduced its new "92" model. It featured a 3,100-square-inch windshield and 25-inch wide jump seats. Hahn also continued to supply its custom chassis in various configurations to other body builders, such as Saulsbury who completed this heavy rescue in 1985 for Shelton, Connecticut. *Mark Redman*

Hendrickson had refined its 1871-W to be slightly less boxy and with standard wheel well/fenders. Benton, Illinois, received this 55-foot Readi-Tower with 1500-gpm pump, 500-gallon water tank, and bodywork by Towers, who was known for its unique pump panel and body design. Note the strobe light bar recessed underneath the windshield. *Garry Kadzielawski*

Known most for its aerial devices, LTI began marketing its own private label custom fire chassis and non-aerial apparatus. The Olympian featured a unique cab with a sloped front and angular wheel wells, made by Kidron, who, like TCM, was a specialty truck and cab manufacturer. Neffsville, Pennsylvania, operated this 1985 model with 1500-gpm pump, 2200-gallon water tank, and 300-gallon foam cell. *Jeff Mogush*

Mack ceased production of complete fire apparatus in 1984, but continued to offer the venerable CF fire chassis to other body builders, many of which, including Emergency One, took advantage of the Mack reputation and aggressively marketed apparatus on that chassis. Lynnfield, Massachusetts, operated this 1985 model with 1500-gpm pump and 750-gallon water tank. *Joel Woods*

Pierce continued to take over the fire apparatus industry and was now marketing its own private label aerial devices, made for them by Smeal. Monroe, Ohio, received this 1985 model with 1500-gpm pump, 300-gallon water tank, and 75-foot aerial on an Arrow chassis. *Steve Hagy*

The contour, fixed-cab Royale had become Pemfab's top-of-the-line fire service offering. Anne Arundel County, Maryland, operated this 1250-gpm pumper with 750-gallon water tank and Emergency One body-work on a 1985 Royale chassis with fully enclosed, four-door cab. *Jeff Mogush*

Hendrickson jump-started the transition to tilt-cab configurations. Darley completed this 1250-gpm pumper with 1000-gallon water tank on a 1985 chassis for Richton Park, Illinois. The 1871-WT could visibly be discerned by the presence of a front grill, which was necessary for cooling the forward mounted engine. *Garry Kadzielawski*

Sutphen continued to be known for its pioneering tower ladder and was building a nicely designed chassis with exclusive TCM cab and trademark bezels. Newington, Connecticut, received this "TS" 100-foot model with 1000-gpm pump and 300-gallon water tank in 1985. *Glenn Vincent*

Pirsch had become another legendary name that was being left in the dust by the new generation of fire apparatus. Among its last successes was a newly designed cab built by TCM, more in-line with the aesthetic standards of the day. Hartford, Connecticut, operated this 1985 model with four-door cab and "riot proof" middle crew windows. *Mark Redman*

The no-frills Seagrave M model, which was originally intended to compete for military pumper contracts, escaped to the civilian market as the Invader. A large group was built for Philadelphia and several were produced for smaller departments. Warren, Rhode Island, received this 1986 model with 1000-gpm pump and 750-gallon water tank. *Shaun P. Ryan*

Duplex continued to refine its fire chassis lineup. The D-350 Enforcer was now the standard contour cab offering. It featured soft lines and a standard, but generally pleasing appearance. South Holland, Illinois, received this LTI 1500-gpm quint with 300-gallon water tank and 100-foot aerial ladder in 1986. *Garry Kadzielawski*

Emergency One introduced a revolutionary design in 1985. The Hush featured a rear-mounted engine and fully-enclosed cab. Gone was the engine doghouse in the cab, which resulted in a spacious and quiet interior for the crew. East Berlin, Connecticut, received this 1986 model with 1500-gpm pump and 750-gallon water tank. *Mark Redman*

The Spartan Gladiator was among the most heavy-duty fire chassis and available to practically any manufacturer that wanted to build a custom fire apparatus. Short-lived Steeldraulics received its first contract from San Francisco. Two 100-foot tractor-drawn units and two 75-foot quints were built on 1986 Spartan Gladiator chassis. *Chuck Madderom*

Legendary American LaFrance succumbed to the enormous pressure of the new fire apparatus generation and shut down in 1985. It was revived by Kersey Manufacturing and resumed production in 1986 with the Century 2000. In order to save on start-up, the new Kersey/ALF utilized a stripped Pemfab Marquis chassis for the Century 2000 line. *Mike Bakunis*

Federal Signal, the corporate parent of Emergency-One, formed Federal Motors, who was tasked with building the custom chassis for its fire subsidiary and new specialized chassis for the commercial industry. This 110-foot rear-mount on a Hurricane chassis with contour cab was delivered in 1987 to the renowned "O.W.L." volunteer fire department in Virginia. *Joel Woods*

Upstart KME jumped with both feet into the industry by gobbling up some assets of the former Hendrickson chassis division. This marked a period in which certain products would seem interchangeable among several manufacturers for some time. The Firefox, with contour TCM cab, was among KME's first custom fire models. St. Louis would receive fifteen 75-foot LTI quints on 1987 Firefox chassis. *Dennis J. Maag*

Another specialty truck manufacturer, Ottawa Truck introduced its own custom fire chassis with exclusively designed 94-inch wide TCM cab in the mid-1980s. It was used extensively by Beck Fire Apparatus. Such a combination was this 1500-gpm pumper with 500-gallon water tank delivered to Garden Grove, California, in 1987. *Chuck Madderom*

Pemfab had upgraded the "93" Wedge cab and now called it the Premier. The newer style could be differentiated by the cab sloping down to a new shelf-like assembly that contained the head and warning lights. Orange County, Florida, received this 1987 model on which American Eagle completed a 1500-gpm pumper with 750-gallon water tank. *Glenn Vincent*

Pemfab was now marketing its Fire Team Line, which included the Imperial full tilt cab. This model would eventually consist of nearly limitless options, from cab configurations, seating arrangements, and raised roof choices. Livermore, California, operated this 1500-gpm pumper with 500-gallon water tank and American Eagle bodywork on a 1987 chassis with four-door cab with raised roof. *Chuck Madderom*

Four-wheel-drive custom fire apparatus had become somewhat of a rarity. However, Colorado was a Mecca for that option. Frisco specified this 1987 Pierce Arrow four-door pumper with 1000-gpm pump and 1250-gallon water tank. Note how the cab was modified with additional sheet metal to accommodate for gaps between the 4x4 components. *Dennis J. Maag*

Pierce introduced the Dash, its second custom chassis, in 1983. Featuring a tilt-cab, it was of cab-forward or engine-forward design, depending on engine choice. Pierce unveiled its first tractor-drawn aerial on the Dash chassis, among a group of 105-footers built for Pittsburgh in 1987 with raised roof canopy cabs. *Kent Parrish collection*

Spartan continued with giving its fire chassis lineup model names in addition to model numbers. The Monarch, with canopy and four-door versions, was now Spartan's standard fixed-cab offering, which was utilized for this long 1500-gpm unit with 3000-gallon water tank and Darley bodywork delivered to Lake Zurich, Illinois, in 1987. *Garry Kadzielawski*

Middletown, Connecticut, specified an American LaFrance Century 2000 with canopy cab for the South End Fire District on which Saulsbury completed this stainless steel 1250-gpm unit with 2000-gallon water tank. The new Century 2000 featured a full width cab with large windshield and rectangular light bezels. *Mark Redman*

The Pemfab Monogram program, which was available with an Imperial tilt-cab, was another option for various manufacturers to customize an apparatus. American LaFrance utilized variations of the Monograph program for its updated Pacemaker series. Lexington, Virginia, operated this 1988 model with 1000-gpm pump and 1000-gallon water tank. *Kent Parrish*

The innovative Young Crusader II was of mid-engine design with the fire pump mounted under the front of the cab, built on a Duplex chassis with the forward portion of the cab being a D-350 style. Optional were side-entry bus style rear crew doors for the enclosed cab versions. This 1988 model with 1250-gpm pump and 500-gallon water tank was operated by Madeira Beach, Florida. *James Brown*

KME continued the 1871-CS cab from the remains of Hendrickson. American Eagle utilized a 1988 model on which it completed this streamlined unit with LTI 85-foot ladder for Wilbraham, Massachusetts. *Glenn Vincent*

FMC also utilized the Pemfab Monogram program for its Commander series of pumpers. The FMC design featured a black fiberglass band around the front of the cab. Hurricane Utah, operated this 1988 model with 1250-gpm pump and 750-gallon water tank. *Garry Kadzielawski*

The heavy-duty Arrow was the chassis of choice for larger Pierce aerials such as this 110-foot platform with 1500-gpm pump and four-door cab for Enfield, Connecticut. *Mark Redman*

Pemfab offered the stripped Marquis chassis for any manufacturer that didn't have the means or desire to engineer and/or build its own chassis. East Coast builder Ranger met half way for its exclusive custom by taking advantage of the chassis portion while constructing its own extruded aluminum cab. West Annapolis, Maryland, operated this 1988 model with 1500-gpm pump and 750-gallon water tank. *Joel Woods*

The new generation of fire apparatus manufacturers began giving commercial chassis a run for their money. The Pierce Dash D-8000 attacked the Ford C-8000 directly with its Caterpillar 3208-T engine and similar components, but in a competitively priced custom package. The D-8000 could be differentiated from the standard Dash by its small, rectangular grille just above the front bumper. *Garry Kadzielawski*

The early Seagrave heavy-duty RA-110 rear-mount aerial ladder was based on the low-profile W model, which had not been updated since its inception. Goffstown, New Hampshire, operated this 1988 model. *Glenn Vincent*

Spartan also supplied FMC for its Commander pumpers with both cab-forward and engine-forward variations. Woodstock, Illinois, received this 1500-gpm unit with top-mount panel and 750-gallon water tank on a 1988 chassis with enclosed cab and "rear entry" cab doors accessible from the top-mount walkway. *Garry Kadzielawski*

In 1988, Spartan pioneered the "Euro-space" concept, which was a fully enclosed cab with no wall separating the front and rear portions, providing for a completely open interior. Saulsbury completed the first unit for Lake St. Louis, Missouri. The "5 Star" rear-mount pumper featured a 1500-gpm pump with raised operator's stand, 750-gallon water tank, and 100-gallon foam cell. *Dennis J. Maag*

In 1987, Simon, a European company, purchased Duplex, who had also introduced the new D-500 Vanguard chassis, which featured a split-tilt cab and offered a multitude of options. Waterford, Connecticut, received this walk-in heavy-rescue with Saulsbury stainless steel bodywork in 1989. *Shaun P. Ryan*

E-One introduced the Cyclone, their third custom offering, in 1986. The fixed cab retained Hurricane contour characteristics, but sat higher on the frame. The four-door cabs often featured full length crew windows that extended well below the driver and officer windows. Weston, Connecticut, operated this 1989 model with 1500-gpm pump and 1000-gallon water tank. *Mark Redman*

The LTI Olympian, with cab built by Kidron, was based on a Simon-Duplex L series chassis. Mehlville, Missouri, received this 75-foot quint with 1500-gpm pump, 400-gallon water tank, and four-door cab in 1989. Note the Olympian also featured front angled driver and office windows. *Dennis J. Maag*

Progressive Phoenix, Arizona, was the E-One "Hush Capitol," with well over one hundred units purchased in various stages. Later batches featured booster reels mounted in the front bumpers. Others included bus-style folding crew doors and raised roofs. This rig was a 1989 model. *David Greenberg*

In 1988, Grumman began development of its own custom chassis for its Aerialcat platforms. After trial and error, HME was chosen as an OEM chassis supplier and TCM built the exclusive low profile Panther cabs. New Milford, Connecticut, received this 1500-gpm unit with 250-gallon water tank and 102-foot ladder tower. *Mark Redman*

KME marketed an Avenger line of pumpers on its Firehawk chassis, which carried over Hendrickson 1871-W characteristics. This 1500-gpm pumper with 1000-gallon water tank was delivered to Oxford, Massachusetts, in 1989. *Glenn Vincent*

Another legend fell when Maxim closed its doors in 1989. In its last several years, the longstanding F model had received a major makeover with TCM providing the fairly standard fixed cab-forward on a Pemfab Marquis chassis. It is believed that the last Maxim to roll out of the factory was this 1989 F model with 1250-gpm pump, 500-gallon water tank, and 30-gallon foam cell for Affton, Missouri. *Dennis J. Maag*

The original KME Renegade was based off the Hendrickson 1871-WT tilt-cab design and KME's top-of-the-line model. Normal, Illinois, received this 1250-gpm unit with 500-gallon water tank, and LTI 55-foot Fire Stix aerial. Early Renegade's featured a four-door enclosure with gasket that fit the original canopy cab rather than a single piece cab. *Don Feipel*

Pemfab marketed its Monogram program as essentially giving a customer or manufacturer the ability to dream up any combination of components. In 1989, Anne Arundel County, Maryland, chose a rear-engine chassis with Imperial styled cab on which American Eagle completed this haz-mat unit with 1250-gpm pump and 400-gallon water tank. *Kent Parrish collection*

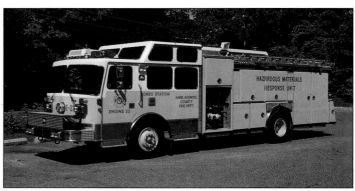

The revolutionary Pierce Javelin featured a rear-mounted engine and front-wheel drive with open cab interior. The cab, chassis, and body were built together and the water tank was situation between the cab and pump. Roughly 100 of these units were built before being phased out. This 1989 model with 1250-gpm pump and 500-gallon water tank was purchased by Silvis, Illinois. *Ron Heal*

In 1988, Seagrave introduced the J model, which would replace the venerable H model. The fixed cab was much refined, but carried over the standard Seagrave cab-forward characteristics. Los Angeles City operated this 1989 JT 100-foot tractor-drawn aerial with open tiller seat. *Chuck Madderom*

Pierce had added the Lance to its expanding lineup in 1986. In essence a top-of-line Dash with multiple chassis, power train, and cab options, it was of engine-forward design with a rear-facing crew bench. Newport, Illinois, received this 1989 model with four-door cab, 1250-gpm pump, and 2500-gallon water tank. *Garry Kadzielawski*

The Spartan Baron offered a mid-engine design with placement behind the cab. The cab could be either a fixed or tilting style. LTI built numerous 100-foot ladder towers on this style of chassis with pumps or as straight truck companies such as this 1989 model for San Diego, California. Note the air intake louvers just forward of the large compartment. *Garry Kadzielawski*

Beginning in the mid-1980s, Sutphen began calling its custom pumpers and single axle chassis apparatus "Deluge" models. The enclosed cabs featured angled rear doors that could also be used for aerials, which required the rear of the cab to be angled for aerial operations. Greenhills, Ohio, received this 1989 model with 1500-gpm pump and 500-gallon water tank. *Kent Parrish*

A trend in the making was the use of two-door custom cabs, which helped create larger specialty apparatus. Homewood, Illinois, utilized a 1989 Pemfab Imperial tilt-cab chassis on which 3-D built this heavy-duty rescue. Rather than wasting empty space over the front wheels, transverse compartments were built in. *Garry Kadzielawski*

The Spartan Gladiator had become one of the premier OEM custom fire apparatus chassis on the market. Spartan had consolidated most of its lineup in its Series 90 designation, whose primary characteristic was the cab windows being dropped down in line with the windshield. Stepney, Connecticut, operated this 100-foot LTI ladder tower on a 1990 chassis with 1500-gpm pump. *Mark Redman*

Chapter 6: **The 1990s**

The 1990s was indeed one of rapid development for the fire service. At the beginning of the decade, Ford announced that the Ford C-Series, *the* most prolific fire apparatus chassis in history, would cease production. New requirements from the National Fire Protection Association (NFPA) in 1991 called for all firefighters to be enclosed, seated, and belted in all new fire apparatus. The age-old tradition of riding the tailboard was over and whereas enclosed cabs were once an option, they were now mandated. These two momentous events opened the door wide open as commercial providers were left salivating, but scrambling to introduce chassis more attractive to the fire service as *custom* chassis were leaving their calling cards all over the table – more interior space and seating for more personnel, more cab and chassis configurations to meet certain needs, factory systems designed specifically for fire apparatus, shorter wheelbases, heavier frames, higher horsepower engines,

and single-source manufacturing.

The increase in safety, comfort, and improved communications proved to be some of the most significant apparatus developments of the decade. New specialty disciplines adopted by the fire service also presented the opportunity for large multi-purpose fire apparatus cabs – such as medical transport, command posts, and rehab centers. All of these factors further opened the door to the custom fire apparatus market as cabs became larger than ever. The multitude of custom options resulted in differentiating cab terms such as short, medium, and long four-door in addition to extended cab. Bigger apparatus, thus larger engines, also spelled out higher pumping capacities with 2000-gpm becoming common in municipal settings. The ideal of maximizing space for man and equipment while minimizing space for machine was seemingly being convoluted into maximizing space for man, equipment, *and* machine. The newer, more efficient engines also required slight running changes in most custom models, especially in regards to grilles and air intakes.

The early part of the decade saw more great fire apparatus names continue to fall. Young and Pirsch both shut their doors for good in 1991 and Grumman's corporate parent inexplicably closed its fire apparatus division in 1992, despite showing a profit, in favor of concentrating on its aeronautical lines. In 1992, Mack discontinued the venerable CF cab-forward fire chassis, ending an impressive twenty-five year run. Pemfab reduced its lineup to just the Imperial tilt-cab and exited the fire business in 1997.

By 1990, Seagrave had replaced both the S and W models with the L model as its single low-profile offering. Featuring an offset roofline, it was Seagrave's first model offered exclusively in a four-door configuration. In 1991, Seagrave unveiled the T model, or Marauder, its first tilt-cab, with an extensive line of options. Variations would include the split-tilt and full-tilt in two- and four-door versions, extended cabs with raised roofs and 10-person seating configurations. With the demise of the Mack CF chassis, FWD/ Seagrave also rescued the popular Baker Aerialscope by providing a heavy-duty J model chassis on which Saulsbury and Marion completed the bodywork. In 1999, Seagrave attempted to reconnect with a customer base that generally had not been able to afford their high-end apparatus. The completely new Flame mid-range chassis was hoped to fill that niche.

E-One introduced its fourth custom chassis offering, the Protector, in 1990. It was a fully enclosed *low cab-forward* with completely open interior made possible by the lower engine doghouse and mid-range power train options. By 1992, E-One had replaced the fixed cab Protector with a completely new tilt-cab (TC) model, as well as offering the heavier-duty Cyclone in fixed or tilt-cab variations in addition to later adding a tilt-cab version of the original Hurricane.

In 1993, E-One added the entry level Sentry custom. This engine-forward tilt-cab featured angular doors that were flush with the cab sheet metal, uncharacteristic of E-One. Generic models also featured grills and air intakes cut directly into the cab. However, in 1996, E-One inexplicably discontinued the Protector TC, both of the Cyclone versions, and the Sentry with a single model – the completely redesigned Cyclone II. This left E-One without a lower level line, which caused the company to retreat and

The Cyclone had transplanted the Hurricane as E-One's flagship custom cab-forward fire chassis. The fixed cab version would remain in E-One's lineup until 1996. Solomons, Maryland, received this 1500-gpm pumper with 750-gallon water tank and four-door cab in 1990. *Joel Woods*

The low-profile Grumman Panther I was utilized for a good number of pumpers, in addition to its primary aerial market. Plainfield, Connecticut, operated this 1500-gpm unit with 1500-gallon water tank. Note the raised roof portions over the jump seats and the light tower sandwiched in the cut out. *Mark Redman*

contract with TCM to build the former Protector/ Cyclone TC cab shell design, which E-One marketed as the custom in its American Eagle economy program. However, E-One continued to play musical chairs with its economy lines over the next several years. In 1997, E-One unveiled a space-age concept apparatus built as a complete unit with aluminum shell covered a composite polymer and "suicide" front doors. It began production in 1999 as the Daytona, which did not prove to be successful.

For 1991, Pierce completely redesigned the Dash. The engine-forward design featured a fully enclosed cab with slightly raised roof over the crew portion,

The Monarch remained Spartan's standard fixed cab offering. Wayne Township, Indiana, utilized a 1990 model tractor with canopy cab, which pulled this big trailer built by Hesse, complete with intakes and pre-piped monitors. It supported the department's Hazardous Incident Response Team. *Kent Parrish collection*

improved legroom up front, and large grille. Initially, it was available only as a two-door model with "rear entry" doors that opened from the crew area into a walkway between the cab and pump panel with a full four-door version soon to follow. The high end Lance would feature running changes throughout the decade. Both the Dash and Lance received major overhauls in 1998 under the "2000" series.

In 1993, Pierce introduced the Saber. It was a mid-range offering that featured a fully enclosed medium four-door cab, which was characterized by all four doors following the contours of the wheel well. In 1995, Pierce introduced one of the most controversial designs since the American LaFrance JO/JOX. The aptly named Quantum featured a protruding nose, roomy cab with air-actuated steps that folded up into the cab, and angular wheel wells. Pierce went global when it was acquired by longtime ally Oshkosh, who enhanced the line with such products as "All-Steer," which enabled each axle to be a steering axle. Continuing its overwhelming domination of the industry, Pierce opened a new facility in Florida before the end of the decade which would make an entire line of economical Contender brand fire apparatus.

KME had established itself as a full line fire apparatus manufacturer with the help of the former Hendrickson chassis lineup. In 1991, KME began to develop its own flair with the Renegade. Two versions were available – one a square cab, the other a softly contoured version. A radical Falcon model was

also marketed. It featured a cab with an extreme front overhang on an International chassis. In 1995, KME introduced the Excel version of the Renegade. A completely new chassis and cab design, it wound up as a stand-alone model versus the Renegade and became the flagship of KME into the new Millennium.

When Grumman closed its fire apparatus division in 1992, HME, who had been supplying Grumman with its proprietary cab and chassis, took both designs and immediately marketed them to the entire fire service while KME acquired the design rights to the Aerialcat line. As it had been established off certain assets from Hendrickson, HME reincarnated the 1871 model name. The familiar cab design would eventually include a multitude of options and versions, including the "P" and "P-2," which enabled HME to be competitive against the other OEMs. In 1994, HME introduced an "SFO" (short front overhang) version of the 1871. It featured a cab that was shortened by two feet by removing the dead space between the front and crew portions and featured a 45-degree cramp angle, which would become a marketable standard for other manufacturers as well. Interestingly, HME also shared the former Grumman Panther I low-profile design with KME. HME marketed it as the Classic while KME utilized it for the Aerialcat.

Struggling to keep afloat amongst the generation, American LaFrance made one final attempt with a new tilt-cab custom called the Patriot. The ungainly Eurospace style cab utilized a Pemfab Marquis chassis. However, it was not enough and the doors seemingly closed for good in 1994. Refusing to die, the American LaFrance brand was yet again resurrected when trucking conglomerate Freightliner announced in 1995 it had acquired the name and assets. The new American LaFrance Eagle would be a premium engine-forward chassis and cab that incorporated all of the modern traits that the brand had failed to recognize in decades past and available to any manufacturer. The first production unit rolled off the line in 1997. However, a complete line of fire apparatus was inevitable. Before the end of the decade, Freightliner and its new corporate parent, Daimler/Chrysler, had gobbled up several independent aerial and body manufacturers and added an economy Metropolitan version to once again be a full line fire apparatus provider.

In the early 1990s, Simon-Duplex completely redesigned its fire chassis lineup to include the Mark

II and Signature Series. The Mark II consisted of the new D-8400. It came standard in a medium four-door format and was characterized by large side air intakes over the wheel wells of the cab. The Signature Series would include no less than seven variations, each with a plethora of options. This line initially featured a cab with sharper angles with later versions featuring more contour. The two most prevalent models were the D-9000, which was a mid-engine design, and the standard engine-forward D-9400. Sadly, Simon began to divest itself of its American fire brands and the Duplex chassis plant was closed by 1998, leaving Spartan to compete against only HME in that segment.

Spartan had become the undisputed leader among the OEM fire chassis providers. As it entered the decade, the majority of its lineup fell into the new Series 90 designation, which was characterized by roomy cabs with large windows that extended down to the windshield line. The Gladiator remained the king among a slew of new tilt-cab models introduced throughout the decade. The traditional cab-forward Monarch was slowly phased out. The Diamond, Metro Star, and Advantage all swapped positions in hierarchy of entry level offerings. Options were limited at times with rather plain grilles and dressing. However, the threesome was often undistinguishable from each other. The Charger was a tilting low cab-forward generally reserved for special applications such as Intra-Cabs.

In 1995, Spartan introduced the GT-One, which was a unique design that shared characteristics of the Silent Knight and Spartan's motor home line. It was a rear-engine design intended to accommodate a rear-mount pump as well. The enclosed cab featured a flat floor which allowed for a completely open interior. Sitting on motor home style wheels, the GT-One only accepted light-duty power trains. The chassis proved to be difficult for most fire apparatus manufacturers to work with and just 30 or so units were completed. In American LaFrance fashion, Spartan also gobbled several independent companies towards the end of the decade which further positioned the company as a full line provider.

Privately owned Ferrara was a new-comer among the fire apparatus ranks who had found overnight fame with its extruded aluminum construction. The company established itself as a custom manufacturer by making arrangements with both HME and Spar-

Clark County, Nevada, was another faithful use of E-One Hush apparatus. Their versions featured E-One's Vista raised roof. E-One also offered an option where the rear compartments were configured to slide back, exposing the rear-mounted engine for ease of maintenance. This 1990 model was equipped with a 1500-gpm pump, 500-gallon water tank, and 40-gallon foam cell. *Garry Kadzielawski*

tan to purchase generic custom chassis which Ferrara would trim and market as its own under the Intruder and Invader pumper series. By 1998, Ferrara had developed its own engine-forward custom chassis and contracted with TCM for an exclusive deluxe tilt-cab called the Inferno and a less dressed up Igniter version, both of which were distinguished by a grill which featured a backlit Ferrara nameplate and angled front windows.

Sutphen was slowly growing from a regional builder into more of a national player with Deluge model pumpers being delivered all over the country as well as its popular aerial platforms. For the first time, Sutphen made a concerted effort to delineate its two main lines. The high-end custom pumpers fell under the Monarch name and tandem axle aerial platforms were dubbed Ambassadors.

The 20th Century came to a close with most of the classic names not surviving. Operation, safety, ergonomics, comfort, and communications were leading fire apparatus development. The progressive new generation of manufacturers was catering to the ever developing fire service and its administrators with a myriad of custom fire apparatus for practically every use, every department, and every budget. While the traditional cab-forward had fully transformed into the enclosed cab engine-forward, the essence of the modern American fire truck was still the same.

The Panther II pumper had become a popular product for Grumman. HME and Grumman teamed to produce well over 300 custom chassis. La Habra Heights, California, operated this four-door 1990 model with 1500-gpm pump and 500-gallon water tank. *Chuck Madderom*

The E-One Hush was also quite adaptable for aerial apparatus. The engine was moved forward between the cab and pump with air vents on the officer's side. This 1990 model with 1500-gpm pump, 200-gallon water tank, and 95-foot ladder tower was delivered to Tinley Park, Illinois. *Garry Kadzielawski*

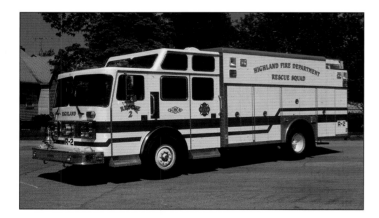

Pemfab chassis were often specified for custom rescue apparatus. Saulsbury completed the body on this 1990 Imperial tilt-cab chassis with four-door cab and raised roof for Highland, Indiana. *Garry Kadzielawski*

In 1990, E-One introduced its fourth custom chassis offering, the mid-range Protector. It was a fully enclosed low cab-forward with completely open interior made possible by the lower engine doghouse and mid-range power train options. Redwood, North Carolina, received this 1990 model with 1250-gpm pump and 1000-gallon water tank. *Shaun P. Ryan*

The Simon-Duplex D-450 was also available for low-profile pumpers, many of which were equipped with smaller aerial devices such as the Tele-Squrt. Pierce completed this unit with 50-foot boom, 1500-gpm pump, and 500-gallon water tank on a 1991 chassis for Plattsburgh, New York. *Ron Bogardus*

Eugene, Oregon, operated this monster 105-foot tractor-drawn aerial built by Pierce, who was still using Smeal ladder assemblies, in 1991. The four-door Lance tractor featured tandem rear axles for better weight distribution. Note the air-conditioning unit on top of the cab, a creature comfort becoming more common with the fully enclosed cabs. *Shane MacKichan*

Grumman ceased the production of fire apparatus in late 1992, after having built scores of Aerialcats, primarily on a mixture of Duplex and HME/Grumman chassis. Aberdeen, Maryland, operated this 1991 Panther I with 1500-gpm pump, 250-gallon water tank, and 102-foot ladder tower. *Joel Woods*

Simon-Duplex also offered a two-door version of its D-500 tilt-cab chassis, which Frederick, Maryland, specified for this tandem axle heavy rescue completed by Saulsbury in 1991. The cab is a true two-door with the body configuration coming over the wheel wells. *Joel Woods*

Pierce was building a niche for rescues and specialty apparatus on its versatile Lance chassis, which offered a multitude of options, such as this 1991 haz-mat unit for Bedford Park, Illinois, which featured a command post in the extended cab with raised roof. *Garry Kadzielawski*

Simon was now vested in LTI in addition to Duplex. The former LTI Olympian style was folded into a new Signature chassis series. The new D-9000 featured a mid-engine design and was available with a unique split raised roof cab, exemplified by this 1991 model with 1250-gpm pump, 250-gallon water tank, and 102-foot ladder tower operated by North Davis, Utah. *Stefan Farage*

The "next generation" Pierce Dash featured a cab that was much larger with more legroom up front and accommodated a wider array of power train options. The new version was an engine-forward fully enclosed cab with slightly raised roof and rear entry doors from a walkway between the cab and pump. Potomac Heights, Maryland, operated this 1991 model with 1250-gpm pump and 500-gallon water tank. *Shaun P. Ryan*

After 101 years of business, the last Pirsch apparatus to be delivered was this fairly standard 1500-gpm pumper with 750-gallon water tank, 50-gallon foam cell, and TCM canopy cab, in 1991 to Osceola, Arkansas. *Steve Loftin*

NFPA now required all firefighters to be belted and fully enclosed in new fire apparatus. This coincided with Seagrave introducing its first engine-forward tilt-cab model, the Marauder, available in full and split tilt configurations with extended cab and raised roof options. Leonardtown, Maryland, received this 1250-gpm unit with 2000-gallon water tank in 1991. *Jeff Mogush*

Another legend came to an end when Mack ceased production of its venerable CF custom fire chassis in 1992. Dobbs Ferry, New York, received this big 1991 model with four-door cab enclosure, 95-foot Aerialscope, and Saulsbury bodywork. *Neal Van Deusen*

KME built the oddball Falcon on an International 3900 chassis, which could accommodate the square cab with unusual, extreme front overhang. Norwell, Massachusetts, operated this 1992 Terminator model with 1250-gpm pump and 500-gallon water tank. *Shaun P. Ryan*

Ottawa also entered the engine-forward genre with its own tilt-cab version; available in both four-door and two-door rear entry configurations. Faithful collaborator Beck finished this 1500-gpm pumper with 500-gallon water tank for Hillsborough, California. *Bill Hattersley*

Pierce continued to build its older style Dash for a short time alongside the new generation. Old Lyme, Connecticut, received this 1250-gpm pumper with 1000-gallon water tank and unique sedan cab reminiscent of Pierce's Fleet Arrow utility version. *Glenn Vincent*

KME had refined its flagship Renegade tilt-cab chassis to feature a version with more contoured characteristics to accommodate the new NFPA requirements. This short wheel-based 1500-gpm pumper with 500-gallon water tank and 30-gallon foam cell was delivered to San Mateo, California. *Chuck Madderom*

Pierce also updated its high end Lance chassis with a new generation look. It also featured more legroom up front and continued to increase the multi-purpose cab options. Warehouse Point, Connecticut, received this heavy-duty rescue with partial walk-in body from the cab on a 1992 chassis with extended cab and raised roof. *Glenn Vincent*

Seagrave continued to offer its fixed cab J model, aka Commander. Grasonville, Maryland, took delivery of this 1992 model with 1250-gpm pump and 1000-gallon water tank. With the new NFPA requirements, the classic canopy cab was a thing of the past. *Joel Woods*

The Spartan Charger was a full tilt model of cab-forward design with side air intakes over the wheel wells. It was often utilized for special applications – such as 4x4 and Intra-Cab configurations, both of which were featured on this 1500-gpm unit with 1000-gallon water tank and Western States bodywork for Douglas County, Washington. *Bill Hattersley*

Aerial towers continued to propel the Sutphen name. Poquonnock Bridge, Connecticut, operated this 1992 TS 95-foot model with 1500-gpm pump and 300-gallon water tank. Note how the rear top portion of the cab is angled to allow for full aerial operations. *Mark Redman*

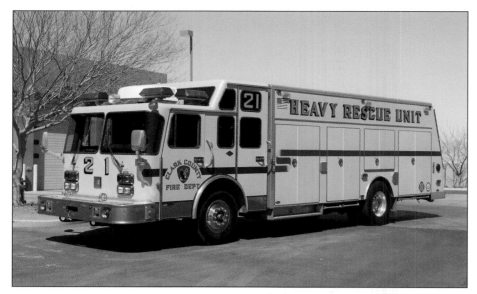

The Silent Knight was Spartan's version of the rear-engine concept, with placement behind the rear axles and an equally quiet, open cab interior up front. It was available for pumpers and specialty apparatus such as this heavy rescue for Clark County, Nevada, a 1992 model with Super Vac bodywork. *Chuck Madderom*

Simon-Duplex had completely redesigned its entire chassis lineup. The Signature Series also included the D-9400, which was the standard engine-forward tilt-cab design. Jennings, Missouri, received this 1993 model with 1500-gpm pump, 750-gallon water tank, and Fire Master bodywork. *Dennis J. Maag*

In 1991, E-One introduced engine-forward tilt-cab versions of both its Cyclone and Protector models. The TC versions, with the Cyclone being the heavier duty of the two, could be distinguished by the presence of front grills and side air intakes. Sykesville, Maryland, received this 1993 model with 1250-gpm pump, 500-gallon water tank, and new generation 75-foot aerial ladder. *Joel Woods*

After Grumman stopped building fire apparatus, HME began offering its chassis and basic cab design to other manufacturers under the familiar 1871 model name, which upstart Ferrara utilized to market its Intruder line of pumpers. Southern Campbell, Kentucky, operated this 1992 model with 1250-gpm pump and 1000-gallon water tank. *Kent Parrish*

After Mack ceased production of the CF fire chassis, the popular Aerialscope was in need of a primary chassis provider. FWD/Seagrave stepped up to the plate with its J model. Riverdale, Maryland, received this 1993 model with 95-foot boom and Saulsbury bodywork. Note the additional sheet metal of the cab to accommodate the necessary components for the Aerialscope. *Jeff Mogush*

HME began to add options to its basic 1871 cab design, including the trends towards larger cabs and raised roofs. Alsip, Illinois, specified an extended cab with raised roof to accommodate interior cabinets and spare air cylinder storage on this 1993 1250-gpm pumper with 500-gallon water tank and Luverne bodywork. *Garry Kadzielawski*

The Saber was Pierce's industry leading 5th custom chassis offering. The engine-forward medium four-door cab and limited power train options allowed for a more economical choice among Pierce's high end models. Blythe, California, received this 1993 model with 1250-gpm pump and 750-gallon water tank. *Chuck Madderom*

Seagrave had replaced its W model with the newly designed L model in the low-profile segment. It was used exclusively for aerial apparatus. Auburn, Indiana, purchased this unit in 1993. It featured a 1500-gpm pump, 200-gallon water tank, and Seagrave's proprietary 105-foot Apollo aerial platform. *Kent Parrish*

The Spartan Gladiator continued to be a preferred OEM chassis for many body builders and heavy-duty fire apparatus. Equipment such as winches and pre-connected rescue tools and reels were becoming common on extended front bumpers. Aberdeen, Maryland, took delivery of this tandem axle unit in 1993 with Saulsbury body and 14-ton crane used for rescue and stabilization situations. *Jeff Mogush*

The Kersey/American LaFrance era came to an end with the unique Patriot split tilt-cab chassis with unusual window compliment. As with the Century 2000, it was built on a Pemfab Marquis chassis. Schuylkill, Pennsylvania, operated this 1994 model with raised roof cab, top-mount 1500-gpm pump, 1000-gallon water tank, and rescue-pumper body. *Kent Parrish collection*

The E-One Protector TC did accommodate heavier power trains than the previous fixed cab design and was often virtually undistinguishable from the Cyclone TC. It was also available for light aerials and heavy rescues, such as this 1994 model with Vista roof and extended cab for Spotsylvania County, Virginia. *Shaun P. Ryan*

KME continued to offer a square cab version of its flagship Renegade engine-forward tilt-cab custom chassis and to be one of the few single-source manufacturers to still offer a short cab with rear-entry crew doors. South Belmar, New Jersey, operated this 1994 model with 1250-gpm pump and 500-gallon water tank. *Scott Mattson*

With the successful next generation design of the Dash, Pierce quickly added a side entry four-door version to the lineup. The slightly raised roof remained standard. Warrenton, Virginia, received this 1994 model with 1250-gpm pump, 750-gallon water tank, and 30-gallon foam cell. Note the array of warning lights. *Steve Loftin*

The Diamond became Spartan's entry-level fire chassis and another engine-forward tilt-cab offering. It featured smaller power train choices and a rather generic appearance with small front grill and vertical side air intakes. Whatcom County, Washington, operated this 1500-gpm unit with 750-gallon tank and 1994 Darley bodywork. *Terry Yip*

Sutphen continued to receive cab shells from TCM, but also, for the first time, began building its own models in its own facilities, becoming a true single-source manufacturer, which was impressive because Sutphen was not considered a large builder. Also added was a tilt-cab, such as this 1994 model with 1500-gpm pump and 1000-gallon water tank for Lutherville, Maryland. *Joel Woods*

Simon-Duplex also offered the D-8400 Mark II Series. The medium four-door featured a larger cab with big, rectangular side air intakes above the wheel wells. It was generally utilized for tractor-drawn aerials. Huntington Beach, California, received this rare quintuple version in 1995 with shortened 90-foot LTI ladder, 1500-gpm pump, and 200-gallon water tank. *Chuck Madderom*

E-One offered the economy level Sentry from 1993 to 1996. The engine-forward tilt-cab featured angular doors that were flush with the cab sheet metal, uncharacteristic of E-One. Generic models also featured grills and air intakes cut directly into the cab. Hampton, South Carolina, operated this 1995 model with 1250-gpm pump and 1000-gallon water tank. *Joel Woods*

Maryland Heights, Missouri, specified a 1995 Simon-Duplex D-9400XL chassis, which featured a slightly extended cab along with the raised roof, for this 1750-gpm quint with 600-gallon water tank, 50-gallon foam cell, and 75-foot LTI ladder. The later Signature Series cabs were characterized by contoured windows as opposed to sharp corners. *Dennis J. Maag*

The GT-One fire chassis shared components with Spartan's motor home lineup. It featured a rear-mounted engine and was intended to accommodate rear-mounted fire pumps as well. Other characteristics included smaller motor home type wheels and seven person cab with flat floor. Frankfort, Kentucky, purchased this 1500-gpm unit with 500-gallon water tank and 1995 Central States bodywork. *Kent Parrish collection*

When Maxim closed its doors, KME gobbled up the remnants and design of the late F model fixed cab and offered it as another version of the Firefox into the 1990s. This 1500-gpm pumper with 500-gallon water tank was completed in 1995 for Riverdale Heights, Maryland. *Joel Woods*

Spartan continued to offer the mid-engine Baron. In addition to the early aerial apparatus, it was also made available for pumpers and heavy rescues. Anaheim, California, operated a group of these pumpers with rear-mounted 1250-gpm pumps, 500-gallon water tanks, and 10-gallon foam cells. Note the mid-ship grill. *Chuck Madderom*

KME had a knack for gobbling up the assets of defunct fire apparatus manufacturers. When Grumman closed its doors, HME and KME both acquired and marketed the basic design of the former low-profile Panther I cab. KME demonstrated this 1996 model with 1750-gpm pump, 400-gallon water tank, and 75-foot Aerialcat, a brand name exclusively secured from Grumman. *Dennis J. Maag*

Ferrara continued to rapidly grow. Still without its own custom chassis, Ferrara also arranged with Spartan to market a Diamond chassis as its Invader model pumper. Dry Ridge, Kentucky, received this 1995 model with 1250-gpm pump and 1000-gallon water tank. Note the Ferrara markings on the Spartan cab. *Kent Parrish*

Although Simon-Duplex offered an expansive Signature fire chassis series, the D-9400 dominated later models. Ledyard, Connecticut, received this low-profile 2000-gpm quint with 200-gallon water tank and 102-foot LTI ladder-tower in 1996. Simon divested itself of the American fire service by 1998 and the Duplex chassis plant was closed, ending the run of a custom fire chassis legend. *Mark Redman*

When E-One discontinued all of its engine-forward tilt-cab models with the introduction of the redesigned Cyclone II, it was left without a mid-range offering, so it contracted with TCM to build the former Cyclone/Protector TC style cab shell and offered it in the economy American Eagle program. South Bound Brook, New Jersey, received this 1996 model with 1250-gpm pump and 1000-gallon water tank. *Scott Mattson*

HME's roots in the commercial and industrial markets enabled it to offer specialty fire chassis, including 4x4 options. The Nevada Division of Forestry maintained a fleet of these 1500-gpm pumpers with 1000-gallon water tanks and 40-gallon cells with Central States bodywork on HME 1871 4x4 chassis. *Garry Kadzielawski*

Pemfab began to streamline its fire chassis offerings in the early 1990s with the Imperial tilt-cab essentially being the sole model and exited the fire business for good in 1996. 3-D completed this 1500-gpm pumper with 750-gallon water tank and 40-gallon foam cell in 1996 for East Fork, Nevada. *Garry Kadzielawski*

HME's version of the former Grumman Panther I low-profile cab was called the Classic and made available to any manufacturer. Ferrara utilized this 1996 model to construct a single axle quint with 65-foot RK ladder, 1500-gpm pump, and 500-gallon water tank for Fishkill, New York. *Ron Bogardus*

Pierce was the first American distributor for the Finish-built Bronto Sky Lift articulating platforms. A heavy-duty Arrow chassis was utilized for this monster 174-foot model, delivered to South Padre Island, Texas, in 1996. The four-axle unit also featured a 2000-gpm pump and 350-gallon water tank. *Eric Hansen*

In addition to Spartan, Smeal utilized HME for custom aerial apparatus, which Kent, Washington, specified for this 105-foot rear-mount ladder built in 1996 on a fairly standard 1871 chassis. Note the bus style mirrors, which had become a trend in the mid 1990s. *Bill Hattersley*

Pierce utilized a Saber cab shell and Arrow chassis, identified by the Arrow grill, for a group of high clearance 4x4 walk-around rescue apparatus built for the U.S. Air Force. A handful of civilian departments were able to piggy-back on the contract as well. This 1996 model went to Andrews Air Force Base. *Howard Meile*

The Spartan Gladiator was also utilized to tractor tillered quints, which had become a regional trend in California. Encinitas received this 1996 model completed by LTI with 1500-gpm pump, 300-gallon water tank, and 100-foot ladder. *Bill Hattersley*

In 1995 Pierce introduced the space-age Quantum, whose appearance remains one of a kind. Available in both standard four-door and short, rear-entry configurations, its characteristics included an unusual nose and air-actuated steps that folded up into the cab. Sault Ste. Marie, Michigan, operated this 1996 model with 2000-gpm pump, 1500-gallon water tank, and 130-gallon foam cell. *Garry Kadzielawski*

In 1995, Freightliner acquired the name and assets of the former American LaFrance and in 1996 introduced a completely new Eagle custom fire chassis under the brand, which would be available to any manufacturer. Westates completed this 1500-gpm pumper with 600-gallon water tank for Pacifica, California, in 1997 on the first production Eagle chassis. *Garry Kadzielawski*

After leading the 1980s into the 1990s with a wide array of popular custom chassis choices, the Cyclone II had become the sole engine-forward flagship of a seemingly misguided E-One. Lake Shore, Maryland, received this 1500-gpm unit with 3000-gallon water tank in 1997. *Joel Woods*

HME complemented its 1871 lineup with an SFO (short front overhang) version. The cab was shortened by two feet by removing the dead space between the front and crew portions and featured a 45-degree cramp angle, which was incorporated into the rest of the 1871 lineup. Westates completed this 1500-gpm pumper with 720-gallon water tank and 20-gallon foam cell in 1997 for Napa County, California. *Garry Kadzielawski*

Cab trends continued towards large, multi-purpose functions and the E-One Cyclone II could be adapted to just about any purpose. Sandy Hook, Connecticut, received this large walk-in heavy rescue with command center in 1997. This configuration typically featured an entry door on the officer's side with a large window on the driver's side. *Glenn Vincent*

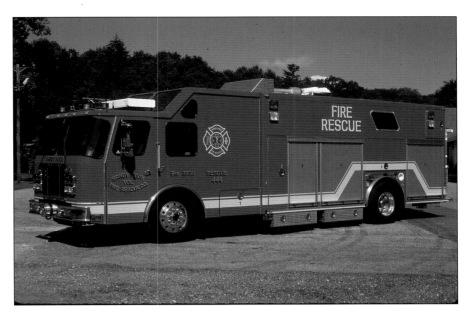

The KME Excel was an entirely new model, redesigned from the ground up, essentially the first of KME's own design and engineering, considering the Renegade's ties to assets purchased from Hendrickson. This 1998 model with 1250-gpm pump, 750-gallon water tank, and 40-gallon foam cell went to Center Township in La Porte, Indiana. *Garry Kadzielawski*

E-One took over as the North American Bronto Sky Lift distributor from Pierce. This 167-foot model with eight axles, unheard of in the North American fire service, was purchased by Calgary in Alberta, Canada, in 1997. It was built on a Hurricane TC chassis, which dictated that it was now available in a tilt-cab format in addition to the original fixed cab configuration. *Shane MacKichan*

The KME Excel was also available in a low-profile format, which essentially replaced the hold-over design acquired from Grumman and shared by HME. It also featured a wide array of options with split raised roof portions now extending over the driver and officer as well. Frankfort, Illinois, received this 1997 Aerialcat with 1750-gpm pump, 500-gallon water tank, and 100-foot heavy-duty ladder. *Garry Kadzielawski*

The Seagrave Marauder split tilt-cab could also be had in a two-door version and was available for other body builders to build on as Seagrave did not specialize in rescue-type apparatus. Rescue 1 completed this tandem axle unit for Waterbury, Connecticut, on a 1997 TC chassis. *Kent Parrish collection*

In 1998, Pierce completely redesigned the Dash, calling it the "2000." In conjunction with new parent Oshkosh, Pierce also offered "All-Steer," which consisted of each axle being a steering axle. Tracy, California, received this 1998 Pierce Dash 2000 with All-Steer, 2000-gpm pump, 500-gallon water tank, and 105-foot ladder. *Shaun P. Ryan*

The Spartan Advantage overtook the Diamond as Spartan's entry level custom fire chassis. It generally featured a plain front grill, air intakes cut directly into the cab, rubber fender liners, and no middle crew windows. General Safety completed this 1500-gpm quint with 400-gallon water tank and 75-foot Aerial Innovations ladder in 1998 for Three Rivers, Michigan. *Kent Parrish*

Pierce also completely redesigned the Lance in the 2000 series. Essentially, it differed from the Dash by remaining a split tilt-cab rather than full tilt and a true engine-forward while the Dash motor compartment slightly encroached into the rear portion of the cab. Downers Grove, Illinois, received this 1998 Lance 2000 with 1500-gpm pump, 200-gallon water tank, and 100-foot platform. *Don Feipel*

In 1998, Ferrara introduced its own custom engine-forward tilt-cab chassis. The top-of-the-line Inferno featured an exclusive cab shell built by TCM. It was distinguished by a grill which featured a backlit Ferrara nameplate and the angled front windows. An Igniter version featured fewer interior frills. Santa Paulo, California, received this 2001 Igniter with 2000-gpm pump and 750-gallon water tank. *Chuck Madderom*

Copper Mountain, Colorado, requested that Sutphen build a 4x4 pumper in 1998. Included was a unique new top-side-mounted panel for the 1500-gpm pump, pioneered by a group including Sutphen, which kept the operator on the side of the apparatus rather than on a walk-way, but still out of traffic. *Dennis J. Maag*

A Pierce Quantum pumper-tanker was truly a large apparatus. It sat high. It was imposing. The Tohono O'odham Nation Native American reservation in Sells, Arizona, purchased this 1998 model equipped with a 1500-gpm pump, 3000-gallon water tank, and All-Steer. *Garry Kadzielawski*

The success of the new American LaFrance Eagle custom fire chassis led Freightliner to gobble up independent body manufacturers and aerial providers to offer a complete fire apparatus line. This tractor-drawn rig was completed in the Becker plant in 1999 for Reno, Nevada, and featured a 105-foot Aerial Innovations ladder. *Garry Kadzielawski*

The space-age E-One Daytona was built with an aluminum shell covered by a composite polymer. Another unique feature was the "suicide" doors that hinged to the B posts. Approximately 10 units were built. Garrison, Kentucky, received this 1999 model via East Lake, Florida. It was equipped with a 1500-gpm rear-mounted pump, 500-gallon water tank, and 30-gallon foam cell within the enclosed body. *Kent Parrish*

The Dash was one of two models, with the Saber being the other that Pierce could equip with four-wheel-drive. Lisbon, Maryland, received this 1999 model with 1000-gpm pump and 500-gallon water tank in 1999. Note the additional sheet metal surrounding the front wheel wells. *Jeff Mogush*

In 1999, Seagrave introduced an economy level custom chassis. The Flame featured a unique, square look with side windows situated high, stamped front grille, and recessed head and warning light assemblies. This rig served as a demonstrator model. It did not prove to be successful and just a dozen or so were produced. *Eric Hansen*

In 2006, Pierce introduced the Velocity and Impel custom chassis, both of which featured a plethora of ergonomic and safety features for firefighters, which had become both mandated and requested by those in the 21st Century fire service. Russell, Kentucky, received this 2007 model with 2000-gpm pump, 300-gallon water tank, and 95-foot mid-mount platform. *Kent Parrish*

Chapter 7: The New Millennium

The new Millennium has proven to be quite challenging for not only fire apparatus manufacturers, but the fire service as a whole. As the first decade came to a close, the nation's economy was the worst it had been since the Great Depression. Traditional big city fire departments were faced with lay-offs and closing stations/companies, not to mention an inability to replace outdated/worn out fire apparatus. As a result, the fire apparatus industry was faced with a 25 to 30 percent reduction in new orders. Many of the big names resorted to spending more money on marketing "budget buster" apparatus.

To further complicate the industry, the EPA invoked two major rounds of engine emissions standards that forced custom fire apparatus manufacturers to redesign models to accommodate compliant engine specifications, which resulted in the price of custom chassis skyrocketing. Rather than comply, some venerable engines simply disappeared from fire apparatus. The 2010 EPA standards were the final nails in the coffins of the Detroit Diesel Series 60, Cummins ISM, and complete Caterpillar lineup. Detroit Diesel would exclusively side with the two-headed Oshkosh/Pierce monster for new models while Cummins would be the savior to everyone else.

Rather than simply accommodate the new engines, manufacturers took the opportunity to completely redesign their cabs and chassis, complete with advanced safety features such as airbags and roll protection, suspension and braking improvements, multi-plexed electronics, ergonomics, and "one-touch" operations. The new Millennium began with trends still leaning towards multi-functional units such as rescue-pumpers and quintuple combinations. Specialty apparatus such as Urban Search & Rescue and haz-mat units began to more commonly utilize custom chassis and cabs. Developing tactics touted technology such as compressed-air-foam-systems (CAFS). However, as the first decade came to a close, a division arose – a growing number of departments began to revolt against complexity and wanted traditional apparatus that were simple to operate and maintain.

Preference had completely shifted towards the engine-forward style and manufacturers were not able to justify keeping a faded concept in their lineup. The new Millennium began with the Seagrave Commander, the Pierce Arrow, and the E-One Hurricane providing life support for the traditional cab-forward concept. However, another momentous paradigm shift had occurred in the fire service and the vast majority of all custom fire apparatus chassis now fell into the engine-forward category. Thus, as the first decade came to a close, while Seagrave, Pierce, and E-One had attempted to sustain the traditional cab-forward, especially Seagrave with the completely redesigned Commander II, the plug was pulled and the pioneering concept peacefully passed away.

A reborn American LaFrance had completely embraced the modern concepts and had rightfully taken back its place in the upper echelon of fire apparatus manufacturers. Operations from the former plants of the independent body builders gobbled up by its corporate parent had been consolidated and streamlined. The premium Eagle chassis continued to serve as the flagship while the Metropolitan was restyled and an entry level Liberty model was added. American LaFrance also jumped on board with a revival of the mid-engine chassis. However, the brand would yet again fall victim to corporate mismanagement, resulting in notoriously late deliveries and, eventually, bankruptcy. Today the legendary name is once again in grave danger.

The misguidance by Federal Signal of E-One in the late 1990s had resulted in a sullied name and quality control issues, thus lagging sales. In 2002, E-

KME was offering the Excel in multiple configurations, including four-wheel-drive. North Lake Tahoe, Nevada, received several units equipped with all-wheel-drive, including this 2000 model quint with 2000-gpm pump, 300-gallon water tank, 40-gallon foam cell, and 100-foot aerial ladder. *Garry Kadzielawski*

One introduced a breath of fresh air. The Typhoon was their first single-source mid-range custom chassis since 1996. Also refreshed was the Hush, which saw the transition to a mid-engine rather rear-engine design. E-One again toyed with the future with the 2007 unveiling of the all new Quest custom chassis, which has seen increasing sales. However, it appeared that E-One was in dire straights as it was plagued by rumors of its sale, which came to fruition as Federal Signal put it on the chopping block. Fortunately, an investment company, one that seems intent on staying out of the shadow, stepped up the plate and rescued one of the great modern fire apparatus innovators. To date, E-One's future seems to be much more exciting with stronger sales and improved quality.

Ferrara Fire Apparatus continued its relatively shocking rise to rock star status. The privately owned company thrived without the inner turmoil of dollar minded corporate politics and had built a loyal following for its extruded aluminum apparatus. Today, most custom manufacturers with their own proprietary models no longer build on chassis from other manufacturers. Perhaps an advantage, Ferrara will. The Intruder models with HME chassis had been updated to the Intruder 2 and an Ember version, essentially an HME chassis with Ferrara front end, would be introduced. Ferrara will currently also still build on Spartan chassis at a customer's request. In an attempt to compete for New York City's notori-

Becker Fire Apparatus was one of the independent builders acquired by the reincarnated American LaFrance. The Red, White, and Blue Fire District in Colorado purchased this unit on a 4x4 Eagle chassis with 1500-gpm pump, 500-gallon water tank, and dual 50-gallon foam cells. Note the clearance difference between the cab and body. *Dennis J. Maag*

ously exclusive business, Ferrara engineered a completely new Ultra model, which featured a fixed cab-forward. However, New York City continued to favor Seagrave and there was barely any outside interest. The Inferno and Igniter continue to be the flagships of Ferrara, who has since joined the ranks of investment ownership.

HME remains the sole competitor to Spartan in their segment. Both have directed their attention towards being a full line provider. Spartan had gobbled up several independent body builders, resulting in the Crimson Fire group. HME had acquired the legendary Ahrens Fox naming rights and began building complete apparatus under that brand as well as an economical Silver Fox moniker. HME also contracted with Kidron for custom cab shells. HME also completely redesigned its chassis lineup, which is still available to any manufacturer, with the flagship 1871 model transforming into the high end "Spectr." Today, HME uses Marion for cabs and has begun building the higher end 1871 in house.

Spartan carried over several of its models from the 1990s into the new Millennium, with the most expansive fire chassis offering in history. New models among the entry to mid-level range included the Big Easy and dedicated four-wheel-drive versions of the Metro Star were called the Mountain Star and Sierra. The kingly Gladiator was also updated with two distinct versions. The Classic featured a more traditional face while the Evolution presented an edgier appearance. Today, even Spartan has greatly streamlined with just the Metro Star and Gladiators in its engine-forward lineup. In similar fashion to what HME has done for Ferrara, the Rosenbauer America group and Smeal have taken advantage of Spartan by acquiring exclusive designs which they've marketed as their own "customs." The Rosenbauer Commander AT features a decidedly European flair while Smeal pushes its more subtle Altair and Sirius versions. A new, increasingly popular offering is the Furion, which is more of a low cab-forward design that has found a niche in custom ambulances in addition to fire apparatus.

KME has undoubtedly cemented itself among the upper echelon of today's fire apparatus manufacturers with a full line of products. Both the Renegade and Excel cab styles have been phased out in favor of the all-new Predator, which in part came about because of the new EPA engines emissions requirements. Today, the Predator is the sole cab offering from KME, but offered in several versions from entry level to high end. KME has also embraced an increasing trend of "Severe Service" apparatus, which have features more conducive to high call volume, urban departments such as simpler electronics and durable interiors. KME also pioneered a "Flameshield" cab that featured window protection systems and insulated aluminum construction that could briefly protect crews from a 2000-degree wildland "burnover."

Still family owned, Sutphen has been able to thrive as well. The company has transformed from a regional, niche manufacturer into a full line provider with the pumper business surpassing that of the famous aerial platform line. With the Sutphen pumpers having been primarily high end, a welcome addition was the economical Elite Series with TCM cabs. This line evolved into today's popular Shield Series, which maintains cost effective TCM cabs coupled with modular body construction. Sutphen also unveiled the radical Imperial. Completely uncharacteristic of the company, the unusual design featured a cab that bowed out in the middle, flush grille, and recessed light assemblies. However, the flagship remains the restyled high-end custom cab shared by the single rear-axle Monarch and tandem rear-axle Ambassador chassis.

Seagrave remains the oldest continuous fire

apparatus manufacturer, dating back to 1881. For any company or industry, this is an impressive feat, accomplished by knowing its boundaries and concentrating on quality over quantity. However, once successful in this manner, a reversal could be detrimental, which Seagrave would find as it became just another portfolio of an investment company – yet again a fate not ultimately beneficial to a legendary fire apparatus manufacturer. In 2004, Seagrave introduced its first entirely new fire apparatus chassis in over a decade. The Concorde was shockingly similar to the ALF Eagle as they were both designed by the same man. However, it was poorly received. Also unveiled was a refreshed mid-level model called the Attacker, which remains in the lineup today with a completely redesigned Marauder II.

Much the way American LaFrance paced the early fire apparatus industry from motorization into the cab-forward era, Pierce, possibly in more dominating fashion, is the undisputed fire apparatus giant of today. Over the first decade of the 21st Century, Pierce has arguably introduced more innovation, primarily dependent on custom chassis, than any period in fire apparatus history. With the venerable cab-forward Pierce Arrow nearing the end of its run, all of Pierce's subsequent custom chassis would be of the engine-forward style. In 2002, the Enforcer was introduced. It was situated above the Saber in hierarchy and shared the same basic cab shell as the Dash, but with fewer options and limited power trains. A year later, the Arrow name was revived in the form of the engine-forward XT, Pierce's version of a high call volume, urban fire apparatus. In 2006, Pierce surprisingly began to phase out the Enforcer, Dash, and Lance in favor of a completely new model. The Velocity and a mid-range Impel version not only accommodated the new EPA compliant engines, but boasted to be "designed for firefighters by firefighters" and featured optional "One-Eleven" mirrors that extended out and down from the roof line, yet another bus influence – one nearly seventy years after the original conception. Pierce further influenced fire apparatus design with its PUC (Pierce Ultimate Configuration), which featured a lowered pump that was engaged unconventionally and that allowed for a more compact design – on each of Pierce's custom chassis.

Much like earthquake prediction, fire apparatus analysts have been barking for decades that Ameri-

E-One, who had provided a handful of tractors for LTI aerials, jumped with both feet into the age-old tractor-drawn aerial tradition, which was making a comeback. San Bruno, California, received this 2000 model with 100-foot aluminum ladder and Cyclone II tractor. *Shaun P. Ryan*

Spartan carried the mid-engine Baron over into the new Millennium. Tempe, Arizona, operated this 2000 model with Saulsbury bodywork. It featured a rear-mounted 1250-gpm pump, 500-gallon water tank, and 40-gallon foam cell. Note the pre-connected attack lines carried on the extended front bumper. *Garry Kadzielawski*

can fire apparatus design is due to embrace European flair and become smaller, cheaper, and more efficient. However, short of roll-up compartment doors and reflective striping, very little European influence has been comparatively seen. The American fire service is fiercely traditional and that will never change. This may be reflected in the rigs as well. The progression of fire apparatus since the horse-drawn era has been truly amazing, yet as *"American as apple pie."*

The tilt-cab version of the E-One Hurricane had become much preferred over the standard fixed-cab. This 95-foot platform with big 2250-gpm pump and 500-gallon water tank was delivered to Chicago Ridge, Illinois, in 2001. However, the style had run its course and with new EPA emissions standards later in the decade, the Hurricane was discontinued in the American market. *Garry Kadzkielawski*

The Pierce Contender custom, which was made in Florida, had become an extremely popular series. Essentially sharing the same cab shell as the Wisconsin-built Saber, it featured fewer frills and a stamped grille. Flagler County, Florida, operated this 2001 model with standard 1250-gpm pump and 1000-gallon water tank. *Kent Parrish*

The basic 1871 continued to be HME's flagship model. It was utilized by manufacturers big and small, such as this 1500-gpm pumper with 850-gallon water tank built by Spencer in 2001 for Watervliet, Michigan. *Garry Kadzielawski*

KME offered a Panther version of its Excel, which was simply a stripped down version with lighter power train. Frankfort, Illinois, received this 2001 model with 1500-gpm pump and 500-gallon water tank. *Garry Kadzielawski*

American LaFrance offered a "low boy" version of its premium Eagle chassis. "Straight" trucks on single rear axles had become relatively uncommon. However, cities like Jacksonville, Florida, and Indianapolis, Indiana, were both users of 75-foot models from LTI. *Bob Milnes*

HME no longer offered the Classic low-profile chassis of Grumman design. Instead, the 1871 design was modified with a notched roof. Chicago Heights, Illinois, received this 2002 model with 2000-gpm pump and 300-gallon water tank. It featured Smeal bodywork and a 100-foot ladder-tower. *Garry Kadzielawski*

The Metropolitan was the modern day version of American LaFrance's Pioneer. It featured more square features than the premium Eagle and a slotted grille. Sterling, Colorado, purchased this 1250-gpm unit with 2500-gallon water tank and 75-gallon foam cell built in the Becker plant in 2002. *Garry Kadzielawski*

The Pierce Saber had become a popular chassis for rescue and specialty apparatus. Serving those functions didn't require a heavy-duty chassis for high call volume life, but served custom functions as needed. San Bernardino City, California, purchased this 2002 model for an Urban Search & Rescue vehicle. *Chuck Madderom*

The new Rosenbauer America group consisted of the General Safety and Central States brands. Rosenbauer made arrangements to customize a Spartan chassis and cab with European flair and market it as their own Commander AT model. Perth, New York, specified this 2002 model with fully enclosed top-mount pump module and rescue-pumper body. *Joel Gebet*

The Aerialcat remained a popular line for KME and was primarily featured on the Excel custom chassis. Purcellville, Virginia, received this 102-footer on a 2002 low-profile version with split raised roof, 1250-gpm pump, and 300-gallon water tank. *Mike Sanders*

The Mountain Star was one of two four-wheel-drive chassis offered by Spartan. It was essentially a mid-range Metro Star with additional sheet metal covering the chassis and components. Note how the cab angles up to the bumper. Lucketts, Virginia, purchased this 2002 model with Saulsbury body, 1500-gpm rear-mounted pump, and 750-gallon water tank. *Mike Sanders*

The fixed-cab Seagrave Commander, or J model, had seen some running changes since its 1988 introduction. One in particular was the additional cooling required for the newer engines, resulting in a tunnel running from the rear doghouse in between the driver and officer to a front grille. Mariemont, Ohio, received this 2003 model built to New York City specs. *Kent Parrish*

E-One combined with Saulsbury to completely redesign the chassis and body style utilized for the Bronto Sky Lifts. This 2003 model on a Cyclone II chassis for University City, Missouri, featured a 2000-gpm pump, 300-gallon water tank, and 100-foot version of the Bronto. *Dennis J. Maag*

HME had become the only OEM that would engineer an Intra-Cab on its chassis. This 2003 model for Snohomish County, Washington, had two distinctions — it was reported to be the last custom Intra-Cab and the last apparatus built by Western States. The rig was equipped with a 1500-gpm pump, 1000-gallon water tank, and 20-gallon CAFS. *Terry Tip*

In 2002, E-One introduced the Typhoon chassis, which was a welcome breath of fresh air as it was their first mid-range single-source offering since 1996. It could be differentiated from the Cyclone II by the presence of side air vents. This 2003 model with 1250-gpm pump and 1000-gallon water tank was delivered to Dillsboro, Indiana. *Kent Parrish*

The Excel continued to be the flagship chassis of KME. Hagerstown, Maryland, received this 1500-gpm pumper with 500-gallon tank in 2003. Custom cabs were starting to be outfitted with accessories such as brow-mounted and recessed flood lights. *Jeff Mogush*

Additional accessories finding their way on the custom cabs of the day were roof mounted light towers that extended up into the air and consisted of a bank of flood lights similar in fashion to those on football fields. Mid County, Missouri, purchased this 2003 Pierce Dash. The light tower was protected by a box on top of the raised roof. *Dennis J. Maag*

The Spartan Gladiator continued to be the king of OEM fire chassis. It was preferred by departments that designed new rigs such as rescue-pumpers from the ground up and let out bids to any manufacturer who would build their dream. Edgewood, Kentucky, received this 1500-gpm unit with 500-gallon water tank and 30-gallon cell built by Summit Fire Apparatus on a 2003 chassis. *Kent Parrish*

The standard fixed-cab Pierce Arrow had been discontinued as that style had become outdated. The name was revived a year later with the Arrow XT, which was designed for high volume "urban" use. The apparatus was free of complex electrical components and featured a durable interior. Its trait was the air conditioning condensers on the cab roof. Los Angeles City received the pilot model in 2003. *Chuck Madderom*

The Spartan Metro was also available in a Sierra 4x4 version, which was preferred by Riverside County, California, who operated a fleet of them. Clearance was calculated for wildland use. Smeal completed this unit in 2003 with 1500-gpm main pump, 200-gpm auxiliary pump, 500-gallon water tank, and 20-gallon foam cell. *Chuck Madderom*

In 2003, Seagrave recognized the 343 firefighters fallen during the 9-11-2001 attack on the World Trade Center in New York City in conjunction with the complete redesign of the new Commander II fixed-cab. This 1000-gpm squad with 500-gallon water tank featured a commemorative mural donated by Seagrave employees. *Mike Martinelli*

Spartan added the Big Easy chassis to its lineup, another choice in its modern myriad of custom choices. It was situated at the entry-level position, but available with choices bringing it into mid-range. Hillsboro, Missouri, received this 2004 model with 1250-gpm pump, 1000-gallon water tank, and Crimson bodywork. *Dennis J. Maag*

The venerable rear-engine E-One Hush had run its course and was redesigned in conjunction with Saulsbury, now a sister company, in a mid-engine format. This configuration was primarily favored by departments in Arizona. Surprise operated this 2004 model with 1500-gpm pump and 500-gallon water tank. American LaFrance also introduced their version of the mid-engine concept on an Eagle chassis for Phoenix. *Stefan Farage*

In an attempt to compete for New York City's notoriously stringent specifications, Ferrara engineered and built a custom fixed cab model called the Ultra. Engine 26 was assigned this 2004 model with three-stage high-pressure 1000-gpm pump and 500-gallon water tank. Just a handful were built for other departments. *Dan Decher*

Girdwood, Alaska, specified an all-wheel-drive pumper-tanker. KME accepted the task and produced this 6x6 Excel in 2004 with 1500-gpm pump and 2000-gallon water tank. The two-door cab featured extra compartment space and even storage above the front wheel wells. *Dan Decher*

Sutphen unveiled the radical Imperial custom cab, which featured an unusual cab that bowed out in the middle, flush grille, and recessed light assemblies. To date, around a dozen have been produced. Anderson, Indiana, purchased this demonstrator in 2004 with 2000-gpm pump, 300-gallon water tank, and redesigned 100-foot platform. *Chris Allen*

The Marauder continued to be Seagrave's flagship chassis. It also accommodated a new line of OEM aerial platforms provided by RK. The Tahoe-Douglas Fire District in Nevada received this 2004 model with 1500-gpm pump, 300-gallon water tank, and 100-foot platform. *Shaun P. Ryan*

Spartan had given the longstanding Gladiator a much needed makeover and a choice of two faces. The Classic version was the more traditional of the two. It was specified for this two-door model which S & S used in 2004 to complete a 3000-gallon tanker with 1000-gpm pump and 40-gallon foam cell. *Mike Sanders*

Sutphen had generally only offered premium custom fire apparatus to date. The new Elite series provided a mid-range offering affordable to a wider demographic, which really expanded Sutphen sales. Bethel-Tate, Ohio, received this 2004 model with 1500-gpm pump, 750-gallon water tank, and rescue-style body. *Kent Parrish*

Similar to the arrangement with Rosenbauer, Spartan provided a proprietary custom chassis to Smeal, who marketed two versions. The Altair was more customized while the Sirius featured more of a Spartan look, but with exclusive Smeal trim. Hazelwood, Missouri, received this loaded Sirius 75-foot quint in 2004 complete with unusually placed booster reel. *Dennis J. Maag*

American LaFrance constructed this massive Urban Search & Rescue trailer in 2005 pulled by an Eagle custom chassis for Alhambra, California. Such configurations were quite rare in the fire service as specialty trailers were generally pulled by commercial tractors. *Chuck Madderom*

HME was now offering a complete line of fire apparatus after acquiring the rights to the legendary Ahrens Fox name. Also introduced was a "SLe" version of the 1871 that featured a split mesh grille within a painted surround and retro circular headlights. Zoneton, Kentucky, received this 2005 model with 2000-gpm pump, 500-gallon water tank, and 109-foot RK ladder. *Kent Parrish*

KME began phasing out the Renegade and Excel styles with the introduction and production of a completely new Predator chassis. The cab was engineered to accept the looming EPA engine emissions standards, for which all manufacturers would have to make modifications to comply. Liberty Area, South Carolina, purchased this 2005 model with 1500-gpm pump and 1000-gallon water tank. *Dan Decher*

Ferrara had continued its arrangement with HME for mid-range, entry-level custom chassis, which was updated to the Inferno 2 series. This 2006 model was delivered to Charlestown, Indiana, with a 1500-gpm pump, 750-gallon water tank, and 30-gallon CAFS. *Kent Parrish*

With the fire service taking on more specialty services, respective apparatus were becoming larger and larger, often requiring tandem rear axles, once reserved only for aerials and pumpers-tankers. Glendale, California, received this 2005 Pierce Lance Urban Search & Rescue apparatus with extended command cab. *Chuck Madderom*

The all-new Seagrave Concorde was shockingly similar to the ALF Eagle as they were both designed by the same man. The failures of both the Concorde and Flame proved that customers demanded the traditional Seagrave designs. White Meadow Lake, New Jersey, purchased this 2005 model. *Mike Martinelli*

The mid-range American LaFrance Metropolitan now shared the same basic cab shell as the premium Eagle. An entry level Liberty was added to the lineup as well. Skyline, Colorado, received this black over yellow Liberty in 2006 with 1500-gpm pump and 750-gallon water tank. *Stefan Farage*

The less costly Igniter version of the Ferrara Inferno had proven to be the best seller of the two. Most departments had become financially conscious and the Igniter afforded a high-end apparatus without a deluxe interior. This 2006 model with 1500-gpm pump, 700-gallon water tank, and 30-gallon foam cell was delivered to Anchorage, Kentucky. *Kent Parrish*

The P-2 was an entry-level version of the HME 1871 with fewer frills and smaller power trains. HME was also using Kidron for cab shells. Bluegrass Fire Apparatus, an up and coming builder in Kentucky, constructed its second custom unit on this 2006 model for Nebo, Kentucky. It featured a 1500-gpm pump, 1500-gallon water tank, and 30-gallon CAFS. *Kent Parrish*

Pierce updated its Quantum, with slightly redesigned front end, under the "Chrome" moniker. With its roomy and comfortable cab, the Quantum had become extremely popular with departments in the scorching West. North Las Vegas received this 2006 model with 1500-gpm pump, 750-gallon water tank, and 30-gallon foam system. *Chuck Madderom*

The Monarch had become the flagship of the Sutphen pumper line. The heavy-duty chassis shared a similar cab with the tandem axle Ambassador. Mason, Ohio, received this 2000-gpm rescue-pumper with 750-gallon water tank and 30-gallon foam cell in 2006. *Kent Parrish*

In 2006, Pierce introduced the Velocity. The heavy-duty chassis featured an ergonomic cab that accommodated the new EPA compliant engines and was characterized by a small hood below the windshield and exclusive "One-Eleven" bus-style mirrors that came out and down from the roof line. The original demonstrator model was painted black. *Dennis J. Maag*

Madison, Indiana, received this 2007 American LaFrance Eagle with 1500-gpm pump, 300-gallon water tank, and 100-foot LTI platform. Over the next year, ALF would yet again be plagued by simmering problems boiling over. Cash flow issues, poor quality, and extremely tardy deliveries would ultimately result in bankruptcy and to date, a bleak future. *Kent Parrish*

Ferrara continued to creep further up the fire apparatus food chain and had become one of the industry's "top guns." Ferrara also continued to be the beneficiary of Smeal aerial assemblies. This 85-foot mid-mount platform was delivered to Lawrence-Cedarhurst, New York, in 2007. *Joel Gebet*

HME was now marketing its 1871 SFO chassis within its own economical Silverfox line in addition to other manufacturers. Ekron, Kentucky, received this 2007 model with 1500-gpm pump, 1200-gallon water tank, and 40-gallon foam cell. *Kent Parrish*

Pierce introduced the mid-range Enforcer in 2002. Situated above Saber, it essentially shared the same cab shell as the high end Dash and could accommodate a 75-foot aerial, but with limited power train options. The New Chapel Fire Company in New Albany, Indiana, received this 2007 model with 1500-gpm pump and 500-gallon water tank. *Kent Parrish*

Seagrave replaced the mid-range Flame with an updated Attacker version, which has been marketed better and remains in production to date, but still a great minority amongst Seagrave sales. This 2007 model with 1250-gpm pump and 750-gallon water tank was delivered to Greensburg, Indiana. *Kent Parrish*

Pierce apparatus in New York City has generally been a rarity. However, the famous Rescue Company 1 received this tandem-axle heavy-rescue in 2007 on a Pierce Arrow XT chassis with two-door cab. The apparatus was built to the department's stringent specifications. *Joel Gebet*

The refined Advantage had become Spartan's most popular chassis model under the high end Gladiator by the middle of this decade. The Central division of Rosenbauer completed this 1500-gpm pumper with 750-gallon water tank in 2007 for Owensboro, Kentucky. *Kent Parrish*

In 2005, Seagrave completely redesigned their dated tilt-cab design with the all-new Marauder II. As was required of all manufacturers, it met new EPA engines emissions standards in addition to sporting a much more functional cab. Louisville, Kentucky, is one of the few traditional cities to still specify single-rear axle aerial apparatus. This 2007 model featured a 100-foot ladder. *Kent Parrish*

The Evolution version of the Spartan Gladiator presented a meaner look than the traditional Classic with recessed and character features. Maui, Hawaii, chose the Evolution face for this tandem-axle hazmat unit which was completed by SVI in 2007. The apparatus featured a slide out lab, much like slide out modules of high-end recreational motor homes. *Kent Parrish*

Sutphen had redesigned its long-standing aerial platform chassis, where the bucket sat over compartment space rather than the former free-hanging style. Sedona, Arizona, received this 2007 Ambassador with 1500-gpm, 300-gallon water tank, and 100-foot platform. *Garry Kadzielawski*

The Pierce Impel shared the same cab shell as the high-end Velocity, but had essentially replaced the Enforcer as a mid-range choice. Kingsland, Georgia, received this 2008 model with 1500-gpm pump, 750-gallon water tank, and 30-gallon foam cell. *Kent Parrish*

Spartan had begun to streamline its considerable fire chassis line. However, the Furion was added as a modern low cab-forward more in line with a "super-commercial." Becoming more common today as a "custom" chassis for heavy-duty ambulances, it is also utilized for lighter duty pumpers. Jakes Branch, Kentucky, had Wynn Fire Equipment build this 1250-gpm CAFS pumper in 2008. *Kent Parrish*

The compact 75-foot Meanstick had become one of the most popular products for Seagrave in modern times. Pleasure Ridge Park, Kentucky, received this 1500-gpm unit with 500-gallon tank on a 2008 Marauder II chassis. With the tilt-cab style dominating the fire service preference, the venerable fixed-cab J model Commander would soon be discontinued. *Kent Parrish*

Today's streamlined Spartan fire line only includes the high end Gladiator, mid-range Metro Star, and low cab-forward Furion. However, Spartan is still the dominant force in its segment. Hurricane Creek, Kentucky, took delivery of this 1250-gpm CAFS pumper built by Crimson on a 2008 Metro Star chassis with unique two-door cab configuration. *Kent Parrish*

Ferrara took the Intruder 2 concept a bit further with another arrangement with HME in which Ferrara completely trimmed out an 1871 cab with its own flair, including grille and light assemblies. Evansville, Indiana, received the first production Ember model, this 2009 model with 1500-gpm pump and 1000-gallon water tank. *Frank Wegloski*

E-One was beginning to reclaim its spot in the top tier of fire apparatus manufacturers in conjunction with unveiling its latest ultra-modern custom chassis called the Quest, which featured a unique front end and sharp window lines. Glendale, Arizona, took delivery of this 2009 model with 100-foot platform. *Garry Kadzielawski*

HME has taken the somewhat dated 1871 cab and refined its lineup as well. With three levels, the Spectr has become the high-end model with the SFO remaining in its own category. Mokena, Illinois, received this 1500-gpm pumper with 1000-gallon water tank and Alexis bodywork on 2009 HME Spectr chassis. *Don Feipel*

Single rear axle Sutphen mini-towers and ladders have been an extremely popular product line. Today, the line is available with a restyled Monarch cab, which is essentially shared by the Ambassador tandem axle units, but with the upper rear of the cab angled for aerial units. Sellersburg, Indiana, received this 2009 model with 1500-gpm pump, 500-gallon water tank, and 75-foot ladder. *Kent Parrish*

The Pierce Ultimate Configuration (PUC) was a revolutionary concept in which the pump was lowered and engaged unconventionally. The design allowed for a more compact unit with more compartment space. It would be available on each of Pierce's wide array of custom chassis. Hartford, Kentucky, received this 2009 Contender Custom with 1500-gpm pump, 1000-gallon water tank, and 20-gallon foam cell. *Kent Parrish*

Sutphen has transformed into an elite member of today's fire apparatus industry. The more economical Shield Series pumpers with TCM cabs and modular construction have become just as popular as its famous aerial platforms. This 2009 model with 1500-gpm pump and 1000-gallon water tank was delivered to Big Sandy, Kentucky. *Kent Parrish*

More Great Titles From

Iconografix

All Iconografix books are available from direct mail specialty book dealers and bookstores worldwide, or can be ordered from the publisher. For book trade and distribution information or to add your name to our mailing list and receive a **FREE CATALOG** contact:

Iconografix, Inc.
PO Box 446, Dept BK
Hudson, WI, 54016

Telephone: (715) 381-9755, (800) 289-3504 (USA), Fax: (715) 381-9756
info@iconografixinc.com
www.iconografixinc.com

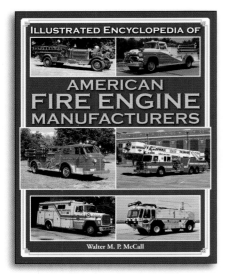
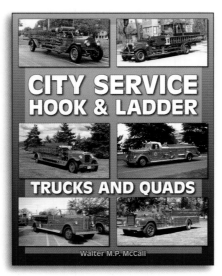
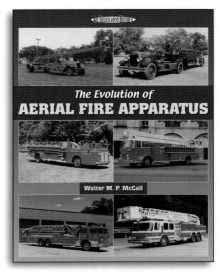
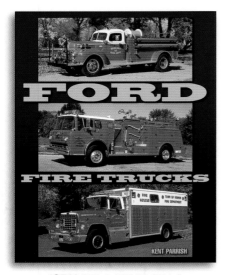
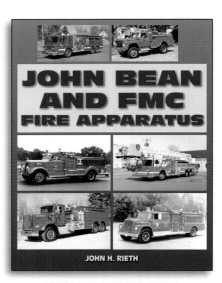